Wheelspin & Smoking Tyres

Wheelspin & Smoking Tyres

A personal photographic record of motor racing
in the 1950s and 1960s

KEITH DUERDEN FBIPP FRPS
with Robert Barker

TRANSPORT BOOKMAN PUBLICATIONS

Published by Transport Bookman Publications Ltd
Unit 26 Murrell Green Business Park, Hook, Hampshire, RG27 9GR, UK
+44(0) 1256 765443
www.chaters.co.uk

Copyright © Keith Duerden
Keith Duerden has asserted the right to be identified as the author of this work

ISBN 978-0-85184-074-1

A catalogue record of this book is available from the British Library
Designed and typeset by Martin Richards
Produced by Roger Bonnet

Printed in China through World Print Ltd

Page 1: *British Grand Prix, Silverstone 1954. Fangio in the Mercedes-Benz W196 'Stromlinienwagen' takes the old Chapel Curve during practice.*

Title pages: *Goodwood, September 1954. Peter Collins at the wheel of the 4.5 litre 'Thin Wall Special' on his way to a win in the Formule Libre Woodcote Cup.*

To David

Best wishes from Nick
& Patricia

Contents

Foreword

Before wind tunnels, racing cars had a sharp end to cut through the air and a body whose only tasks were to cover the working parts and accommodate the driver. Given those essentials, the skilled artisan who created the body could give his artistic imagination free rein. And so, racing cars of the '40s and '50s are beautiful – to me at least – and I am more than happy to be reminded of them. I first encountered Keith Duerden's photographs in early examples of Autocourse magazines of the 1950s. When I met the man himself and saw more of his work it was almost half a century later. I needed no persuasion to help in the task of sorting and identifying his long stored images and so began the journey that has culminated with this book. As you turn the pages, imagine how I felt in seeing these pictures that had been hidden away for so long. It had been both a pleasure and a privilege. If you share my affection for the racing cars – and drivers – of the period, you are in for a rare treat.

Robert Barker

Acknowledgements

I would like to mention a number of people who have, in various ways, helped me along the way. I first met the late Alan R. Smith, fifties motor racing photographer and writer, through the Reigate Photographic Society while I was still a schoolboy. His guidance and encouragement in those very early stages meant much to me. It was my classmate at school, Michael Hall, with whom I began watching those very early post-war meetings who, much more recently, urged me to unearth my photographs for others to see, leading eventually to the publication of this book. To guide my first faltering steps into the digital age, the help from my IT consultant son-in-law Colin English proved invaluable, building my website and helping its launch at the Goodwood Festival of Speed and Revival. It was there I first met motor racing author Robert Barker. The happy coincidence of my need to supplement my hazy memories and lack of records with Robert's willing enthusiasm, his mine of information and gentle insistence to proceed which led to our collaboration. It would be a very different book without his help, if indeed it had happened at all. It is also Robert who supplied all the programme covers and thanks are due to the BARC, BRSCC and BRDC for their kind permission to reproduce them here. And finally, my heartfelt thanks to my wife Gillian for her support as well as bearing with my pre-occupation while putting this project together.

Keith Duerden
www.duerdencollection.com

Introduction

The author, clutching his Leica, stands behind Alberto Ascari on the grid for the 1953 British Grand Prix.

Photograph by Alan R Smith, reproduced with the kind permission of 'The Klementaski Collection'.

Imagine this teenage boy, still at school, in the mid to late 1940s. Two apparently isolated themes are about to come together in a quite unplanned way which will shape his future career and eventually, by a very roundabout route, lead to the publication of this book. His world is only just emerging from the wartime years with all its austerity and shortages. He's been lucky enough to have been too young to serve in the military during the war, yet old enough to have understood something of the significance of that period. He watched the vapour trails overhead during the Battle of Britain, moved to relatives in Lancashire during the worst of the blitz, learned the geography of North Africa, Europe and the Far East following the progress of the war, listened to the Doodlebugs' during lessons in the school air raid shelters and eventually celebrated with everyone else around the bonfires when it was all over.

One day, a year or so later in the 'dinner' hour, he rushes down to the bookshop in the town with some saved pocket money to spend. Browsing, his attention is caught by a book with a photograph of three racing cars on the cover and an exotic sounding author by the name of Prince Chula of Thailand. The pocket money is spent and over the next few days that boy becomes aware of another world. The book is entitled 'Road Racing 1936', with a sub-heading 'being an account of one season of B. Bira, the racing motorist'. More pocket money will be saved and spent as other accounts of Bira's exploits through the later '30s are published in such books as 'Wheels at Speed' and 'Blue and Yellow' as well as Bira's own book 'Bits and Pieces'. It is an interesting comment on the times that book publishing itself is still very restricted and that book was 'produced in complete conformity with the authorised economy standards

ROAD RACING
1936
PRINCE CHULA
OF THAILAND

'Bira'

Hero of my schoolboy encounter with the Bira books, 'Bira', or in full, Prince Birabongse Bhanudej Bhanubandh of Siam, here at Silverstone to drive a works Gordini in 1952.

From the mid thirties until the war stopped racing in 1939, Bira built his reputation driving ERAs in voiturette racing with great success. After a few races in 1935 with Riley and MG, he took delivery of his first ERA just days before taking it to Dieppe where he came second, followed by another second place in the Prix de Berne. An impressive debut!

1936 saw the formation of the 'White Mouse Stable' run by his cousin Prince Chula. Now with two ERAs, named 'Romulus' and 'Remus', Bira's career took off, an outstanding victory at Monaco being just the start.

As with many of the prewar racing drivers, Bira was soon back in action after the hostilities and had an early win at Chimay in 1947 with a Maserati 4CL. His partnership with Chula ended late in 1948 and he linked up with the Enrico Plate team, driving a Maserati 4CLT which was later converted to the 4.5 litre OSCA of 1951. Seasons followed with Gordini and Connaught before finally returning with Maseratis, first an A6GCM and then a 250F. After some success in minor events, he retired in the middle of '55 following his final win at Ardmore in the New Zealand Grand Prix.

'Remus' *today being prepared in the Goodwood 'Revival' paddock.*

to book production war economy standard.

That boy was of course me, and it just happened that motor racing was taking its first, tentative steps after the war. Initially, because racing on public roads was not permitted on the mainland and with pre-war tracks such as Brooklands no more, motorsport was at first restricted to sprints and hill climbs on private estates. But in Ireland, the Isle of Man and Jersey where more relaxed rules applied, circuit racing on public roads began again, as indeed it did all over the Continent.

As well as the books I was reading, there were wonderful reports in the weekly magazine 'The Motor' of those early post-war races across the Channel. Written by Rodney de Burgh Walkerley under his pseudonym 'Grand Vitesse' and brilliantly illustrated by Bryan de Grineau's atmospheric drawings, they also captured my imagination. I can still 'see' in my mind a wonderful drawing of this new driver over from Argentina in a full blooded drift during the Albi Grand Prix, probably in 1949. His name was Fangio. At the same time, many of the drivers with whose names I had become familiar while reading about their pre-war exploits now featured again, their racing careers having been put on hold during the conflict. I shall be forever grateful to the gentleman who ran the station W H Smith bookstall for saving, under the counter, my copy of 'The Motor' to collect each Wednesday on my way to school – a further reflection on the times. For a younger reader today it must be difficult to imagine, with magazine racks heaving under the weight of all the different motoring publications!

Quite coincidentally, my interest in photography also began. That all started when my older brother bought a camera. He was serving in the

RAF on air/sea rescue launches, first around Cromarty Firth and then off the coast of Malaya. Seeing the photos he sent home made me want to take my own pictures and soon, with yet more pocket moneysaved, I had my first simple camera, an Ensign Fulvue, quickly followed by developing and printing equipment and materials. I was well and truly caught by the photography 'bug'. It seemed natural that these two keen interests should be combined, and I went along to early sprint and hill climb meetings. First, the 1947 Brighton Speed Trials, followed in '48 with a sprint in the grounds of Luton Hoo and then the Brighton Hill Climb in Stanmer Park, where an 18 year old youngster called Stirling Moss won his class in his second ever event. This was followed by my first circuit race meeting – the original Goodwood event in September 1948, Moss again a winner. Just 16 years old, I went with my classmate Michael Hall, making our way by train to Chichester and bus to the circuit, the first of many trips to the circuits together.

Later, I was at Silverstone to see the very first Formula One Grand Prix at Silverstone in 1950, won by Giuseppe Farina, when the beautiful 158 Alfa Romeos swept the board and there again the following year when they were beaten for the first time as Gonzalez gave Ferrari their very first GP win.

I was hooked! From then and through the early to mid 50s, I went to many of the main meetings at Goodwood, Crystal Palace and Silverstone plus a memorable trip to Le Mans in 1953 when the C-type Jaguars came first, second and fourth. All without track passes – something simply not possible today – just this young chap honing his skills as he made his way

in his chosen career. I had no thoughts at all about any potential future interest for these shots and I was somewhat casual about the care of them, most of those early shots no longer exist. At the time, they were serving their purpose in giving me practice in all the skills I would need and were then put on one side while I moved on to the next challenge. Not much thought to personal safety either, frequently standing right on the edge of the track. After the bigger events, I usually posted a selection of prints to 'Autocourse', the leading motor sport magazine at that time and they usually picked some for publication, thus earning my first picture credits and modest fees.

National Service intervened in the two years 1951/52, but even then, I was lucky to serve in the photographic branch of the RAF, based at Benson in Oxfordshire, working on aerial survey photography. Prior to that posting, I was on a ten week course at the RAF School of Photography, Wellesbourne Mountford in Warwickshire, my first formal training, as up until then such photographic skills as I had acquired were self taught. While at Wellesbourne, through the spring and early summer of 1951, I managed to get to a Prescott hill climb and the International Trophy at Silverstone and then, while at Benson, if a weekend pass coincided with an event, I would try to be there, sometimes hitchhiking – easy in uniform in those days – or otherwise by train, coach or bus until a little later I acquired a 125cc two-stroke motorbike which gave me more flexibility.

Along the way, that first camera was traded up via a folding 120 camera and a Kodak Retina to, in 1953, a rather secondhand Leica 111c, with which the majority of the '50s pictures in this collection were shot. After the RAF, a career in professional industrial photography quickly evolved, at first with The Monotype Corporation, until, in 1956 when I was recruited by Mobil Oil as their new staff photographer. Immediately, my life moved in other directions, not only my career, but marriage, house building and the arrival of a young family all certainly changed my priorities and I had little time, money or opportunity to exercise my camera at the tracks. It was not until 1964 that I made a return, this time to Brands Hatch for the first Grand Prix on the newly extended full GP Circuit, a race which had no less than five drivers who all either had achieved F1 World Champion status or, in John Surtees' case, would by the end of the year.

In the eight years I had been away, the whole face of Grand Prix racing had changed. The days of the front engined car had gone, and following the pattern inspired by Cooper, new teams such as Lotus and Brabham had emerged, all now with the engine behind the driver. Ferrari and BRM were still there of course, but the Maseratis, Gordinis, Vanwalls and Connaughts had all retired from the scene and a whole new intake of drivers had taken over, mostly somewhat younger than those I had been watching in the '50s. Occasionally, my work at Mobil would take me back to the tracks, as in 1959 when I went to Dundrod in Northern Ireland to photograph John Surtees in his last year on two wheels and winning his seventh championship with the MV Agusta team. Another time was in 1981/2 when Mobil sponsored the Williams team – the Alan Jones and Keke Rosberg years.

The illustrations in this book form a very personal record of these years and while not pretending to be a comprehensive survey of the period I hope they go some way to recapturing the atmosphere as well as illustrating the differences from today of those very special times. My earliest surviving photograph is of Stirling Moss in his second competitive year driving his Cooper at Goodwood in 1949. I was fortunate enough to see in action the first nine Formula One World Champions – Farina, Fangio, Ascari, Hawthorn, Brabham, Phil and Graham Hill, Clark and Surtees – together with many of their contemporaries. I hope they will bring back good memories for others of my generation who were around in those days as well as being of interest to more recent motorsport enthusiasts and photographers, enabling comparisons with today's more complex and restricted times.

Looking back, my time at the circuits proved to be an important grounding for my future, leading to my career in professional photography. Skills such as assessing and reacting to a situation, composing the shot and timing just the right moment to release the shutter in days when everything on the camera had to be thought through in advance and manually controlled – no auto focus or exposure and certainly no motordrive. Perhaps it all seemed natural to me at the time and maybe I took it all for granted, but I realise now just how lucky I was to be gaining this experience – my 'learning curve' – at a time when the likes of Fangio and Moss were gracing the tracks.

Keith Duerden

The late 1940s and into the '50s

GOODWOOD, EASTER 1949

Leading the way in the postwar generation of British drivers, Stirling Moss, who after a successful first year in a Cooper 500, upgraded in 1949 to this Cooper which he raced in both 500cc and 1000/1100cc classes, changing engines between races. With the larger engine, Moss won the Second Easter Handicap and in September, the Madgwick Cup. During that summer, Moss made his first foray on to the Continent with this car, taking it to Lake Garda. The Italians had not seen anything quite like this funny little car with its engine behind the driver – to them it was a joke. But after he came third in his heat and then the final, easily winning the 1100cc class and being beaten only by the bigger engined Ferraris of Villoresi and Tadini, their amusement turned to admiration and Moss had taken another important step in his career.

This early in his career, Moss has yet to adopt his trademark arms outstretched, relaxed style at the wheel, adopted by him after he saw Giuseppe Farina racing at Zandvoort a little later in the season – 'my first sight of him influenced my formative years more than anything else'. He has also not yet begun to claim the number 7 as 'his' competition number.

While I was on holiday by Lake Garda in 1991, I found that an event for period cars, the 'Circuito del Garda', was to be run over the same course just along from where I was staying. Too late to get a photograph of him, I was delighted to discover that the event was to be opened by none other than Luigi Villoresi, a brief sighting some 38 years after I had last seen him at Silverstone. He died in 1997 at the age of 88.

I was just 17 years old and still at school when I shot this, the earliest surviving photograph of those early events I attended. My camera at the time was a folding 120 with a top marked shutter speed of 1/125th of a second but I doubt if it managed much better than a 1/80th even on a good day so I got plenty of panning practice!

Two British drivers to make a major impact in the late forties and early fifties were Bob Gerard and Reg Parnell. The two raced pre-war and quickly re-established themselves as competition started up again, Gerard driving meticulously prepared ERAs while Parnell was able to acquire the latest Italian machinery, first a Maserati 4CLT and then a Ferrari 500/625. Parnell became the Aston Martin team manager after giving up driving and later ran the Yeoman Credit and Bowmaker teams. He died at the age of 52 from peritonitis after a routine appendix operation. Gerard retired from single seater racing in 1957 but continued in club events with a Turner sports car into the '80s, finally becoming an entrant.

Top, left to right: *Bob Gerard with his wife and daughter, a rare engine failure as a piston lets go in the '51 Goodwood Festival of Britain Trophy and with fellow ERA driver Brian Shawe-Taylor.* **(Below)** *Parnell in serious discussion with prewar driver and doyen of the racing fraternity, Earl Howe on the Goodwood grid and in action with his 4CLT Maserati in 1951.*

For me as a spectator at the very first Goodwood meeting in '48, the highlight was the great duel between these two in the main race, Parnell's Maserati, faster on the straights just beating the older but better in the corners, Gerard ERA by 0.4 of a second.

BRANDS HATCH, APRIL, 1950

I had already been to Brands Hatch in its motorcycle grass track days, taken by my brother on the pillion of his Triumph Speed Twin. This was the very first race meeting for cars after the original simple kidney shaped circuit was surfaced in 1950, running anti-clockwise as before and this view is of the bend at the foot of Paddock Hill, the Druids loop not being added until 1954 when the direction was also reversed to clockwise. Don Parker in his 500cc JAP engined Parker Special leads a trio of Coopers into the climb up Paddock Hill on his way to winning the first ever car race at the circuit. Note the spectators cars in the background! The basic programme cover indicates that the meeting was organised by 'The 500 Club'.

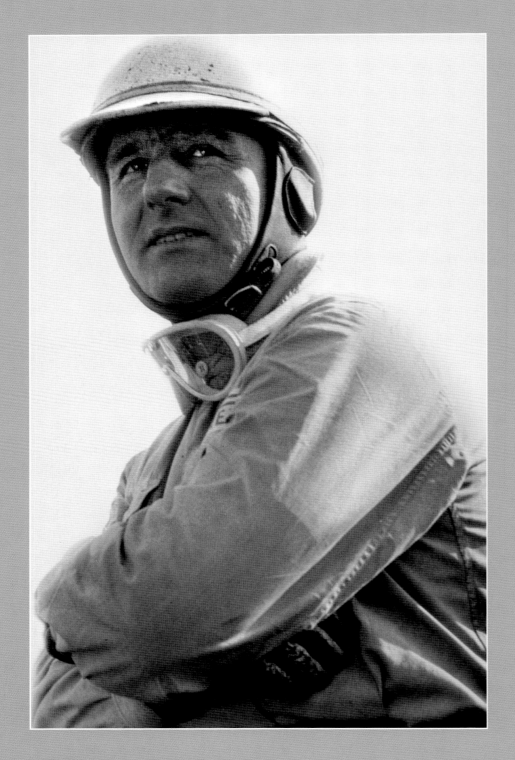

Giuseppe Farina

The first Formula One World Champion, 1950

1950 saw the inauguration of the F1 World Drivers Championship, to be run over six Grand Prix in Europe while also including the Indianapolis 500, a position the American race held in the championship until 1960 although playing no significant part in it. That first year was dominated by the Alfa Romeo team with its three star drivers, Giuseppe Farina, Luigi Fagioli and Juan Manuel Fangio. Fagioli had been brought in to replace Consalvo Sanesi who had been injured in the Mille Miglia and at 53 was the oldest of the three, with Farina at 43 and Fangio a mere youngster of 38.

The very first championship race, the British and European Grand Prix was held in May at Silverstone and attended by The King and Queen. As expected, the 158 Alfa Romeos ran away with it, Farina coming in first, thus setting off on his way to securing his place in the history books as the first Formula One World Champion. Fangio's car expired a few laps from the end leaving second place to Fagioli with Britain's Reg Parnell third as Alfa's guest driver in the fourth team car.

Over the following years, Farina continued to feature in the championship, coming fourth in '51, again with Alfa Romeo and then second in '52 and third in '53, driving for Ferrari. He had a reputation as a forceful driver and it was best not to get in his way. He eventually retired after a succession of crashes only to lose his life in a road accident in 1966.

I attended that 1950 British Grand Prix, travelling to Silverstone by coach and spectating in the braking area for Stowe Corner. I had yet to learn how easy it could be to get closer to the action even without track passes and this shot of Farina was taken in 1953 just after he has driven to third place in the Grand Prix, completing 88 laps in 2hrs 50mins. By now 46 years old, he seems remarkably fresh and relaxed on the grid for the Formule Libre Trophy to be run just following the GP – merely another 17 laps. He won, driving the 4.5 litre Ferrari 'Thin Wall Special', from the two V16 supercharged 1.5 litre BRMs of Fangio and Ken Wharton. Farina also set the first official 100mph lap of Silverstone in this race.

Juan Manuel Fangio

World Champion, 1951 and 1954 to 1957

One of the greatest Grand Prix drivers of all time, many would say the greatest, Fangio missed out on the 1950 World Championship by just three points but asserted his authority in '51, still driving for Alfa Romeo and beating the emerging challenge from the Ferrari team led by Alberto Ascari as well as his own Alfa team mates.

I was privileged to be a spectator at the '51 British Grand Prix when Fangio battled with his good friend and compatriot, Jose Froilan Gonzalez driving the 4.5 litre Ferrari, the larger unsupercharged car emerging triumphant to give Ferrari their very first F1 GP win. Over the season however, Fangio prevailed before the Alfa Romeo team withdrew at the end of the year. His move to Maserati should have provided the main opposition to Ferrari in 1952 but in the event he missed the whole of the season due to a broken neck sustained in a non-championship race at Monza.

By 1953 I had made some contacts and was finding my way around on the 'inside' at the circuits and over the next four seasons had the good fortune to observe at close-quarters and photograph the master at work as he went on to take four more driver's titles, with Mercedes-Benz, Ferrari and Maserati.

Collecting autographs was never of interest to me yet something made me take this print of Fangio at Silverstone **(right)** to the next time I saw him, which was at Goodwood where he kindly signed it for me. It is the only driver autograph I collected in those days, but if there had to be just one, I guess I could not have made a better choice. His helmet and goggles are not his usual racewear and it has been suggested that he may have arrived at the circuit on a borrowed motorcycle. It is certainly possible – just the sort of thing that could have happened in those days before motorhomes and helicopters made the avoidance of traffic jams so easy.

(Left) *Although often referred to as husband and wife, Fangio was not married to Beba, his constant companion throughout his career. She had a husband back in Argentina where divorce was not possible and they then separated when he returned home on his retirement as a driver.*

INTERNATIONAL TROPHY SILVERSTONE, MAY 1951

The final of the International Trophy looked more like a swimming gala than a motor race. As the grid lined up for the start of the International Trophy race, the heavens opened. With cars spinning off all round the circuit and the timekeepers unable to see through the spray, the race lasted just six laps before it was abandoned, Reg Parnell in the 4.5 litre unsupercharged Ferrari 'Thin Wall Special' being declared the winner, ahead of the usually all conquering works 1.5 litre blown 158 Alfa Romeos. Perhaps it was an omen, for at the British GP two months later, Gonzalez in the works Ferrari beat Fangio's Alfa into second place, marking the end of the Alfa Romeo post war supremacy and the arrival of Ferrari as a force in Grand Prix racing.

I hitch-hiked from my RAF camp to Silverstone, the last stage with a young couple in a majestic pre-war saloon and they very kindly suggested I meet them after the event for a lift back.

Top: *Fangio in the 158 Alfa Romeo and* **(below)** *the winning 'Thin Wall Special' driven by Parnell.*

Returning through the car park in the deluge, wading at times through shin deep muddy pools of water, I apologised for the state I was in and felt I really should not get in their lovely car. They were in much the same condition however and insisted I return with them, an offer I accepted with gratitude, chilled and soaked as I was. It was altogether another matter to get my uniform into something presentable before the next morning parade!

Stirling Moss

Stirling Moss, in the F2 HWM, gets a push from HWM (Hersham & Walton Motors) founders John Heath, nearest camera and George Abecassis. By the time I took this photograph at the Goodwood September 1951 meeting, Moss had spent two seasons travelling all over the Continent as one of the works drivers for the team gaining more valuable experience. Although the HWMs were underpowered compared to the Ferraris and other continental opposition they encountered, they flew the flag and paved the way for those British teams that followed on with increasing success.

Later in his career and after works drives with Maserati and Mercedes Benz, Moss finally fulfilled his patriotic wish to drive a British car at the top level with the Vanwall team in 1958, helping them, with four wins, to the newly introduced Formula One Constructors Championship.

Below Superstition is not uncommon in sport and Moss's number 7 was seen as often as possible on all types of car that he drove. Even the painted lucky horse-shoe had seven nail-holes.

I feel very lucky to have caught this shot – it must have been early in his claim to the number and I was certainly not aware at the time I took it, just how much it would come to be identified with him.

1952

GONZALEZ IN THE MIGHTY V16 BRM.

Swiss driver Baron Emmanuel de Graffenried, winner of the 1949 British GP driving a Maserati, here relaxing in the Silverstone paddock.

Tony Rolt (right, dark glasses) gives Duncan Hamilton a push start in the HWM, Silverstone, May 1952.

INTERNATIONAL TROPHY, SILVERSTONE, MAY 1952
A real mix of competitors at Stowe: De Graffenried,
Maserati, Parnell in a Cooper-Bristol, Duncan Hamilton's
HWM and Northern Ireland driver Bobbie Baird's Ferrari 500.

A distinguished career and a future World Champion (left)

Mike Hawthorn burst on to the scene at Goodwood, Easter 1952 with two wins and a second place, driving the new Cooper-Bristol. Here, he looks less happy in the Silverstone paddock while his father searches for gremlins in the engine during the May meeting. In July with this car, he finished third in the British GP and by the end of the year, he had made enough of a name to be snapped up by Ferrari for 1953. And he didn't always wear a bow tie!

Louis Chiron, near the end of his long driving career, at Silverstone in 1952 to drive this works Gordini. As early as 1928, he won the Marne GP at Reims and the Italian GP at Monza driving Bugattis, followed up in '29 with victory at the Nurburgring in the German GP. From there, right through the '30s he featured regularly in the top placings including a Monaco win in '31 as well as several second places there in his home race.

Right: *Beneath the Union Flag is the monogram 'LM' signifying that this works HWM Alta is driven by Lance Macklin, a stylish driver who gave the team a win in the Daily Express International Trophy, encouraging despite the absence of the Italian works cars.*

Alberto Ascari

Formula One World Champion, 1952-1953

World Champion for Ferrari and son of the famous 1930s Alfa Romeo driver Antonio who was killed at Montlhery when Alberto was seven. He was taken under Villoresi's wing and developed into a Grand Prix winner in '51 with Ferrari. In the following two years he won nine GPs in succession. Moving to Lancia in 1954, he had no luck, culminating in his dive into Monaco's harbour in '55. Days later he died testing a sports car at Monza.

I was on holiday in Lugano in 1955, and caught the train for a day in Milan. Returning in the evening, I noticed another passenger reading a newspaper – the headline read 'Ascari Morto'.

Below: *Ascari, on the right, with two of his Ferrari team mates in 1952, Piero Taruffi and Giuseppe Farina, chatting together before practice for the British GP at Silverstone.*

British Grand Prix

Lined up behind the pits, ready for action, the three works Ferrari 500s to be driven in the 1952 British Grand Prix at Silverstone by Ascari (15), Farina (16) and Taruffi (17). Its just a thought, but if this had been a line up by the German Mercedes Benz team, they would have been in numerical order.

Always looking for ways to get my camera closer to the action, bearing in mind my lack of a photographer's pass, I found that tickets could be bought to the viewing area above the pits and watched the racing from there, an inexpensive extra which gave me a different viewpoint.

Through 1952, the Ferrari team had four of Italy's great drivers, Giuseppe Farina, Luigi Villoresi, Piero Taruffi and Alberto Ascari.

These three shots make an interesting comment on the informal nature of those days as well as the sense of team spirit which then prevailed.

Notice too, the absence of a separate pit lane, a simple white line being the only demarcation from the track.

Top left: *Taruffi listens to Farina making a point to one of the team mechanics while Villoresi helps with the paperwork.*

Top right: *Farina and Ascari, obviously enjoying each other's company, take a stroll in front of the pits and* **(left)**, *Ascari, Farina and Villoresi chat together in the paddock.*

Pit stops took rather longer in the '50s than they do today. Farina brings his Ferrari 500 in for a plug change. As the bonnet goes back on, the mechanic at the front steadies the starter motor ready to fire up the engine again. This stop put Farina back to a sixth place finish, spoiling a Ferrari clean sweep.

A Ferrari one two – Ascari and Taruffi head into their pits and a warm welcome at the end of the 1952 British Grand Prix.

This was Ascari's third win in a run of nine consecutive GP victories, six in 1952 followed by three more at the start of '53 – a run broken only by Hawthorn's win over Fangio in the French Grand Prix at Reims. As a sign of things to come, it was the Cooper-Bristol of Mike Hawthorn which came in third here behind the two Ferraris.

Taruffi chats to his mechanic before the start. He began his motorsport career as a successful motorcyclist and later combined a role as Gilera's team manager while he was a works F1 and sports car driver for Ferrari.

Above: *Ken Wharton, driving on the day for BRM and non-starting for Frazer Nash in the sports car race, talks with the Duke of Kent.*

Above: *Victor in the following Formule Libre race, Piero Taruffi in Tony Vandervell's 'Thin Wall Special', the third modified Ferrari to carry the name. This 375 model mixed it with the BRMs on many occasions. He was penalised for a jumped start in the Formule Libre race and put in a spirited drive to win. This, just after coming in second to Ascari in the Grand Prix.*

Right: *Gonzalez in the mighty V16 BRM. In 1952, Formula 2 was promoted to World Championship status following the withdrawal of Alfa Romeo – BRM was thought to be no serious opposition to Ferrari. The 'Thin Wall' and BRMs were left to have their own private war in the Formule Libre races.*

Luigi Villoresi, not engaged in the Grand Prix, urges on his Ferrari team mates.

Ascari and Ferrari team manager Ugolini congratulate Villoresi on coming second to Taruffi in the Formule Libre race. But it was still a defeat for the works car by the British modified Ferrari.

Enthusiastic team mates Ascari and Farina, still in their oil stained clothes from the Grand Prix, urge Villoresi on to greater efforts.

From Silverstone's very early days, a feature of both the main meetings, the International Trophy event in May and the Grand Prix in July, was the very full race programme. From 500s to two sports car races covering up to 1500cc and over, touring cars and Formule Libre as well as the main event for Grand Prix cars.

What has changed since the early '50s is that many of the top GP drivers would also find and take drives in the other categories. Fun for the drivers – as well as a little more in their 'kitty' – and added value for the spectators.

On a glorious summer day, sports cars rounding Stowe corner in the early '50s. Note the sand filled oil drums marking the inside line of the bend.

This delectable line up of early '50s pure sports racing cars are being readied for the Le Mans type start of a 'Production Sports Car Race'. Works Jaguars and Aston Martins tended to dominate and there was little surprise that Stirling Moss won the May '52 event in a C-type Jaguar. If his Grand Prix career was yet to take off, he had certainly made an impression as a sports car driver.

GOODWOOD, EASTER 1952

Now into my second year in the RAF, I managed to get to Goodwood for the Easter '52 meeting and witness the newly installed Paddock Bend, known universally as the Chicane **(above)**. Duncan Hamilton locks his Lago-Talbot's rear wheels chasing Tony Rolt's ERA Delage and Graham Whitehead in ERA R10B with George Abecassis following up in the HWM.

Below left: *At the same meeting, a close encounter with the 'Pampas Bull', Jose Froilan Gonzalez, there to drive the 4.5 litre 'Thin Wall Special', winning the libre event with great panache.*

*At the September meeting, Gonzalez had switched to BRM and he had two wins in the V16 car. His team mates were Parnell **(above)** and Wharton and they came 1-2-3 in the Daily Graphic Trophy, the only clean sweep ever for these cars. Father of the BRM, Raymond Mays **(left)** said 'this was the result for which we had waited so long. It had come too late'.*

Following his sensational 1952 season, Mike Hawthorn started 1953 as a Ferrari works driver and delivered handsomely at the Silverstone International Trophy, winning his heat and the final. Here, at the start, he mixes it with Louis Chiron, OSCA (16), Ken Wharton, Cooper Bristol (36) and Harry Schell, Gordini (4).

1953

INTERNATIONAL TROPHY, SILVERSTONE, MAY 1953

NOW, HOWEVER DID THAT GET THERE?

Wandering round the Silverstone paddock at the May International Trophy meeting seeking out subjects for my camera, I was vaguely aware of this photograph being set up and then, moving on, thought no more about it. Until the next morning, that is, when I was greeted by a friend from my RAF days – we had been demobbed together earlier in the year. 'Hello, Keith, I knew you were here, you're in today's Giles cartoon'!

An unconventional greeting, to say the least. On buying the Daily Express, all was revealed and there I was playing a 'bit part' in a Giles cartoon! Giles himself is top centre in dark glasses and, knowing he had a mobile caravan as a studio in the paddock, I sought him out and asked him if he would mind signing my copy.

The heading 'Now, however did that get there?' might just as well apply to me!

CRYSTAL PALACE, MAY 1953

A new circuit for London, as the Crystal Palace reopens on the 25th of May, 1953. The Coronation Trophy race for Formula Two cars sees Leslie Marr, Connaught (18), Bill Aston, Aston Butterworth (25), Jack Fairman, HWM (6), Torrie Large, Alta (9) chasing five others (including Collins, Moss and Rolt) under the bridge.

Right: *Stirling Moss, following his patriotic wish to succeed by driving British cars, had a torrid time with a special Alta-engined car built by a team led by John Cooper of The Autocar. Abandoning that project, Alf Francis and his crew built in two weeks this 'standard' Cooper T23 with Alta power with which he won the London Tropy at the second Palace meeting in July. The car proved to be fast but fragile.*

Below: *The second meeting on 11th July at the Crystal Palace circuit saw a win for Tony Rolt in Rob Walker's Connaught A3 ahead of Roy Salvadori's works car.*

Below right: *The superbly prepared Cooper Bristol of 'Mr Bob' – Bob Gerard – came home third in the London Trophy.*

LE MANS 1953

LES 24 HEURES DU MANS 1953
PROGRAMME OFFICIEL

Donnant droit au numéro spécial de « MOTEURS COURSES »

Prix : **200** francs

Somehow, I had kept in touch with my school's English master, who happened to own a Red Label Bentley and was a member of the Bentley Drivers Club which had organised a trip to Le Mans. Luckily for me, they had been unable to sell the last ticket and I was asked if I would like to join them – silly question really! I therefore found myself being chauffeured up to London in the Bentley, then a flight from a very basic Heathrow to Paris and coach to Le Mans, my first trip abroad. We stopped on the way for a very French lunch and only arrived just in time to take our grandstand seats for the start. It was a hot day and with a fine view of the famous Dunlop bridge, I watched the early laps from the shade before exploring the 'Esses' and Tertre Rouge. Spot the sun hats made from folded newspapers – sad that highly skilled self-taught origami has been replaced by baseball caps.

In the pits is the Gordini shared by Harry Schell and Maurice Trintignant. This all-French team (half French in Schell's case) finished a highly creditable sixth in a field of the highest quality.

Early Saturday evening and the first pit stop for the winning car. On the pit counter, watched by team manager Lofty England (in dark shirt), drivers Tony Rolt and Duncan Hamilton confer while mechanics refuel and check vital life-signs. Note the 'plombeur', wearing beret, waiting to reseal the fuel tank. There seems to be an unhurried air about the process.

The classic lines of the C-type Jaguar, caught in the fading light of Saturday evening as Tony Rolt heads into the night shift. This car, chassis XKC051, was a lightweight car with disc brakes which went on to a post-works career with Ecurie Ecosse.

Duncan Hamilton brings the winning Jaguar he shared with Tony Rolt across the line to win the 24 hour race. They completed a record 2540.58 miles at an average speed of 105.85mph.

Right: A spruced up Tony Rolt rushes to greet a somewhat oil-stained Hamilton as the crowds gather round.

Early on Sunday afternoon, I was given the party's one and only pits pass and found a place in the empty Ferrari pits (they had all retired) next to the Jaguars and was right there in the scrum of well-wishers and photographers when the three works Jaguars triumphed, coming in first, second and fourth. Tony Rolt takes his place on the car to share the moment with co-driver Duncan Hamilton on their historic win. Note the shattered windscreen.

Time to enjoy their personal achievement as well as that of the team, Peter Walker and Stirling Moss.

A clearly delighted Stirling Moss is greeted by Jaguar chief William Lyons (right) and (left) team manager 'Lofty' England as he brings the car home. With co-driver Peter Walker, they came in second, only 29 miles behind the winner.

Finishing in fourth place to complete the Jaguar team triumph, Ian Stewart and Peter Whitehead. Only the American Cunningham of Phil Walters and John Fitch gaining a fine third place spoiling a clean sweep for Jaguar.

THE BRITISH GRAND PRIX, SILVERSTONE, 1953

For 1953, three of the previous year's Ferrari team, the Italians Ascari, Farina and Villoresi have been joined by British driver Mike Hawthorn. In the centre, a young Bernard Cahier, at the beginning of what was to become a distinguished career in motorsport photojournalism, listens intently to Ascari.

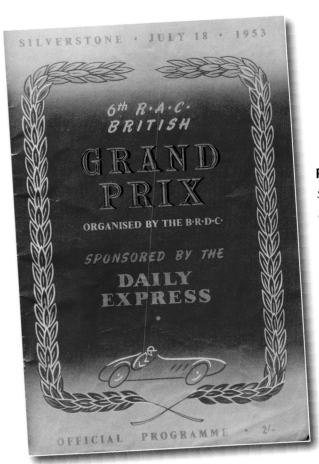

Right: *Ascari drinks, Gonzalez smiles and Farina speaks with his hands. Maserati driver Gonzalez seems to be amused as the two Ferrari team mates appear to be having something of a disagreement. Perhaps the harmony of 1952 is under temporary strain?*

Below: *Harry Schell, on the third row of the grid for the Grand Prix, ponders his prospects,*

Below: *Schell again, talking with Baron de Graffenried in the paddock and (right) Maurice Trintignant, looking calm and collected awaiting the start of a practice session in the second works Gordini.*

Above: *The French Gordinis of Harry Schell (left) and Maurice Trintignant (right) flat out in the 'old' Woodcote corner. Never quite a match in performance to the Italian works cars, they were however an important player in the make up of early to mid '50s grids.*

Supporting the '53 Grand Prix, the Sports Car Race had a quality line up of Aston Martins, Jaguars, with two Cunninghams and a Ferrari over from the USA plus assorted HWM, Frazer-Nash and a Kieft.

Of the early Ecurie Ecosse drivers, the two Stewarts, Jimmy and Ian (unrelated) were the stars. Jimmy enjoyed considerable success in his C Type Jaguar. He was asked to drive for Aston Martin at Le Mans and was injured when the ill-handling fixed-head DB3S crashed. He was due to drive a works D-type Jaguar with Mike Hawthorn at Le Mans in 1955, but a second accident at the Nurburgring just a month before put an end to his racing career. His younger brother Jackie, however, carried the family name to motor racing fame.

Reg Parrnell (above) started the race from pole in this DB3S Aston Martin and went on to win, with team mates Roy Salvadori and Peter Collins in second and third – a clean sweep for the marque. The privately entered Ferrari of American driver Bill Spear came fourth ahead of the two Ecurie Ecosse Jaguars driven by Ian and Jimmy Stewart (right).

Fortissimo! Ferrari team manager Ugolini, on the grid, gives Italian style pre-race encouragement to **(right)**, Luigi Villoresi and **(below)**, Mike Hawthorn, fresh from his exciting victory over Fangio in the French Grand Prix at Reims just two weeks earlier. Perhaps Ugolini went too far in Hawthorn's case who, after a poor start from third on the grid and trying to make up time, 'lost' the Ferrari in a big way coming out of Woodcote, spinning several times on the grass strip in front of the stands and skilfully getting it pointed in the right direction just in time to miss the footbridge at the end of the pits.

Dodging marshals, I worked my way onto the grid by helping to push the Rob Walker Connaught to be driven by Tony Rolt, onto its third row slot. Once out there, I was able to move freely up to the front, nobody bothering about my lack of credentials.

Below: *Autocourse magazine was a quarterly in 1953 and this was the lead page of illustrations to the July GP report which appeared as late as the November issue. Just 21 years old, I was particularly proud to have my shots, which I had posted in on spec, featured in this way but it was a long wait to see them in print and even longer to get paid!*

South American determination – Maserati team mates Gonzalez and Fangio prepare for the battle ahead. Fangio came second and Gonzalez fourth. Coming from Argentina, polo shirts are probably the obvious race wear – note that Fangio's has his initials. Deep, in thought, they seem to be completely unaware of my camera, fortunate, as the shot would have nothing like the impact if they were looking directly into the lens.

*Seconds to go, the front row of the 4-3-4-3 ... grid. On pole, far side, Ascari
(Ferrari), then the Maserati of Gonzalez, Hawthorn's Ferrari and Fangio's
Maserati. The patriotic British fans must have been hoping that Hawthorn
would repeat his success two weeks earlier in the French Grand Prix but it was
not to be. While Ascari and Fangio fiddle with their goggles, Gonzalez and
Hawthorn appear to be quite relaxed.*

The start, with Fangio nearest camera, leading the front row away as he glances across to Ascari and Gonzalez. Hawthorn makes a poor getaway and has dropped back into line with Farina, Villoresi and Marimon starting from the second row.

Complete domination. Fastest in practice, starting from pole and winner of
the British Grand Prix for the second year running, Scuderia Ferrari star
driver Alberto Ascari balancing his Ferrari 500 through Woodcote corner.

Left: *Less than a minute to go before the start of the 'Formule Libre' race. Ron Flockhart's ERA, on the second row, still has a front wheel jacked up while Hawthorn covers his ears.*

Below: *The start of the Libre race sees Fangio, Farina, Wharton and Hawthorn lined up on the front row of the grid. Some supporting race! With the engines started, the scream of the two V16 BRMs of Fangio and Wharton rises above the collective thunder of their rivals. All four of the front row have already competed in the 90 lap Grand Prix lasting nearly three hours - so just another 17 laps to go. Farina in the 'Thin Wall' won the race from Fangio and Wharton with Flockhart's ERA fourth. Hawthorn's Ferrari retired with overheating on the 9th lap.*

Fangio's BRM from pole and Hawthorn's Ferrari appear to have edged out a slight advantage over Wharton and Farina as the Libre race gets under way – all wheelspin and smoking tyres. The tyre marks in the foreground were laid down by Hawthorn's dramatic spin early in the preceding Grand Prix.

Right: Following up from the second, third and fourth rows, a mix of types with G N Richardson's RRA leading, Horace Gould (Cooper Bristol) on the far side, then the ERA of Flockhart who is peering down into the cockpit, Jimmy Somervail (Cooper Bristol) and no. 18, Louis Rosier (4.5 litre Ferrari).

Juan Manuel Fangio drifts the 1.5 litre supercharged V16 BRM through Woodcote corner on his way to second place.

If elegant lines could only lead to success, the BRM should have been a world beater but it was not to be. Not the easiest of cars to drive, or the most reliable, it nevertheless attracted many of the greatest drivers.

Of all my memories, the sight and sound of these beautiful but temperamental cars in full flight and driven by a master like Fangio has to be amongst the most special.

Dr Giuseppe Farina demonstrates his classic 'sit well back, straight arm' driving style that so impressed Stirling Moss, as he steers the 'Thin Wall Special' to victory in the Formule Libre race. On his way to the chequered flag, he set a record fastest lap at 100.16mph, the first official 100mph lap at Silverstone. Not a bad end to a pretty full day for this driver, by now in his mid forties and in the last years of his racing career.

Thin Wall Special

Goodwood in September – a perfect late summer day and continuing with the Formule Libre theme, the heavy machinery has moved to the Sussex circuit for my last meeting of 1953. Lining up on the front row for the 15 lap Goodwood Trophy, from right to left, Ken Wharton's BRM getting a top up, Roy Salvadori's Connaught, the 'Thin Wall Special' driven this time by Mike Hawthorn **(right)**, who would win both libre events and just visible on the far side, on pole, the BRM of Juan Manuel Fangio who can be seen contemplating his main opposition. Just visible over on the far side and leading the second row, sits Stirling Moss in his Cooper Alta that his mechanic Alf Francis built up in just eleven hectic days earlier in the season.

Left: *Amidst a haze of tyre smoke, the two BRMs nose ahead at the start. Hawthorn won for the second time but Fangio retired leaving second place to Wharton with Bob Gerard's Cooper Bristol third.*

Opening the September meeting at Goodwood, the seven lap Madgwick Cup for Formula Two cars. Stirling Moss gets the jump on Salvadori's Maserati 250F (no. 10, on pole), Tony Rolt's Connaught and nearest, Bob Gerard's Cooper Bristol. Sneaking through from the second row, seen between Gerard and Rolt, Les Leston in the diminutive rear-engined Cooper JAP. Salvadori got the better of Moss with Rolt third while Gerard and Leston came in fifth and sixth (below).

Left: *The first Formule Libre race of the meeting was the 5 lap Woodcote Cup. Hawthorn gets away to a great start and leads Fangio and Wharton to the finish.*

Three for the scrapbook

Ahead of its time

1.5 litre supercharged Delage cars dominated the 1926/27 GP seasons. Ten years on, Dick Seaman enjoyed success with one he had modified by Giulio Ramponi, competing against the ERAs and sometimes giving Bira a hard time. Recognising the threat, Prince Chula had this example built up from spares for Bira to race. After the war, it moved via the Parnells to Rob Walker who replaced the by now tired engine with one from a crashed E-type ERA. A distinguished history.

Historic car, historic driver

Cliff Davis was one of the great characters of post-war British motor racing. Here he is **(top picture)** in characteristic check shirt, moustache no doubt bristling, he drives the Tojeiro Bristol which inspired the AC Ace and it in turn spawned the mighty Cobra.

He was second to Mike Keen's Cooper Bristol **(above)** in the Norbury Trophy race at the Crystal Palace September meeting – a car which itself had an interesting history. Prior to wearing this sports body, it started life as the single seater Cooper Bristol with which Mike Hawthorn sprang to prominence in 1952.

1954

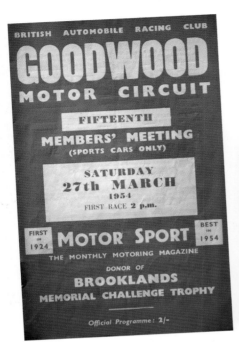

1954 began for me back at Goodwood for the March Members' Meeting, a quite different experience to the higher profile International meetings. The most noticeable feature was the sheer variety of machinery, pre-war cars competing with more recent examples as exemplified by this grid (right): from the 1930s, K W Moore's Bugatti (85) and Hamish Orr-Ewing's Bentley (101) with the two Jaguar XK120s of Tom Kyffin (77) and K Chambers. The enthusiasm of the competitors was shared by a good crowd, some enjoying the spectacle from the control tower **(above)**.

Left: *Elva creator Frank Nicholls raced a Lotus VI at this club meeting. Beside him at the start are Len Gibbs (Riley), Anthony Marsh (Lotus IIIb) and on the far side, Roy Watling-Greenwood and his RWG Ford with which he won two races.*

Clockwise from top left:
J H Bailey's Bentley, Nigel Mann's Alfa Romeo 8C and a group of MGs at the chicane

Another varied grid for a 10 lap scratch race at the March Members' meeting with, far side on pole, the ex Hawthorn re-bodied Cooper Bristol, this time driven by Alan Brown, Tony Brooks in the Le Mans Replica Fraser Nash (No. 29), Michael Head, C-Type Jaguar (No. 22) and (No. 43), Dick Shattock in the RGS-Atalanta. Both Head, centre right and John Coombs with the Connaught ALSR (No. 9), bottom right, won 5 lap scratch races. In this race, Alan Brown made fastest lap and Tony Brooks, top right, was the winner.

Tony Brooks went on to have a short, but very successful Grand Prix career in the late '50s driving for Vanwall ('57/'58) and Ferrari (1959) starting with a shared British GP win with Moss at Aintree, then the Belgian at Spa, German at Nurburgring, Italian at Monza, all in Vanwalls and then, for Ferrari, the French at Reims and Germany again at Avus.

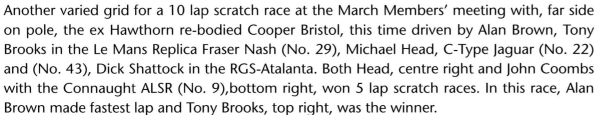

GOODWOOD 1954, EASTER AND WHITSUN MEETINGS

Many of the main competitors turned out for both of these two events – including Ken Wharton and Ron Flockhart in the BRMs, Reg Parnell with his Ferrari, the Rob Walker Connaught for Tony Rolt and Roy Salvadori with the 250F Maserati. Competition for the BRMs came at the Whitsun meeting from the 'Thin Wall Special', this time with Peter Collins at the wheel.

It was not obvious to me at the start of 1954 that the days of 'Formule Libre' were coming to an end and that the Whitsun and September Goodwood meetings were to be the last occasions when I would witness the rivalry on track of the screaming 1.5 litre supercharged V16 BRMs pitted against the lone unblown 4.5 litre 'Thin Wall Special'.

George Abecassis, co-founder of the HWM marque, stands behind Reg Parnell who is raising a smile from Roy Salvadori. On the right is Sydney Greene whose Gilby Engineering entered the Maserati 250F for Salvadori. Smart racing overalls are beginning to make an appearance.

Left: *Lined up for the 5 lap First Easter Handicap for Sports Cars, the two C-type Jaguars of Duncan Hamilton and Tony Rolt with George Abecassis, far side, in a Jaguar engined HWM. The race was won by Jimmy Stewart in an Ecurie Ecosse C-type with Rolt second.*

Rolt was re-united with his 1953 Le Mans winning C-type, 'No 18', now owned by Ecurie Ecosse while Hamilton **(below)** was in the fourth, spare works car. This was later owned for a time by Michael Hall, my friend from schooldays and who had been with me at that first Goodwood meeting in 1948.

In addition to the GP 250F Maserati brought to the meetings by Sydney Greene's Gilby Engineering, this beautiful Maserati A6GCS was also available for Roy Salvadori to enjoy. At the Whitsun meeting, Salvadori came fourth in the 21 lap Johnson Trophy race, giving best to the bigger engined Jaguars which occupied the first three places.

I have to thank the racing team at Rob Walker's Pippbrook Garage, Dorking for the great help they gave me in gaining access to pits and paddock from 1953 through to 1956 both here at Goodwood and also at Silverstone and I dedicate this spread to them.

I always made sure I at least bought a basic entry ticket for each meeting but from there on, fortunately for me, checks on having the right pass tended to be somewhat perfunctory. A pair of mechanics overalls and a willingness to help push the Connaught out on to the grid was often my passport to the start line. The occasional official sweep through the paddock would find me industriously polishing the car and to the best of my memory, I was never challenged. The innocence of youth!

Below: *The Duke of Richmond and Gordon, ardent enthusiast and owner of the Goodwood circuit, listens attentively to Tony Rolt.*

Above: *Despite starting from pole position in the Lavant Cup race, Tony Rolt was forced to retire on the fifth of seven laps. Here, he is seen in discussion with team patron, Rob Walker.*

Right: *Waiting to roll out on to the grid, Tony Rolt chats to John Eason-Gibson.*

Tony Rolt, Connaught (45) leads away from Peter Whitehead's Cooper Alta (39) John Webb's Turner (53), Leslie Marr's Connaught (18) and Alan Brown in the Cooper-Bristol.

In '53, I remember meeting the Pippbrook boys on the approaches to Silverstone as they towed the car in on a trailer – it was before they acquired this luxury vehicle. I was taken in sitting in the Connaught under a tarpaulin!

Bottom left: *From Rob Walker's transporter emerges Connaught A3. Built to conform to the 2 litre Formula Two which had finished at the end of 1953, there were still races to accommodate these cars, including those for the new 2.5 litre Formula One.*

Below: *Tony Rolt was shortly to hang up his helmet for good but here warms up the Connaught in the Goodwood paddock with attentive Pippbrook mechanics in attendance.*

TWO STUDIES

Reg Parnell's Ferrari had started life as a Formula 2 '500' model for Irishman Bobbie Baird. Back at the factory it was updated to '625' (2.5 litre) specification. Now operated by Scuderia Ambrosiana, it gave Parnell his F1 drive for 1954.

Determination and concentration as Reg balances the car under heavy braking for the chicane on his way to winning the Lavant Cup at the Easter meeting **(right)** *and* **(above)** *applying delicate throttle control accelerating away from the chicane and into the pits straight to win the Whitsun Formula 1 race.*

The grid lines up for the 5 lap Chichester Cup race for Formule Libre cars at the sunny Easter meeting with Ken Wharton on pole in the new short chassis Mk II Type P30 BRM. Alongside, Ron Flockhart has the older BRM while Reg Parnell completes the front row in his 500/625 Ferrari – the gap between the BRM and Ferrari should have been occupied by Tony Rolt's Connaught, a non-starter on this occasion due to a sheared magneto drive in the earlier Lavant Cup race. Leading the second row is the 250F Maserati of Roy Salvadorii.

At the start **(left)**, Reg Parnell gets the drop on the two BRMs, with Flockhart lighting up his tyres more than his team mate, although, initially, he eased into the lead before a spin at Madgwick put him well down the field. This left Wharton In the lead which he kept to the finish, chased hard by Salvadori who lost by just 0.4 seconds in an exciting close run to the line. Parnell came third while Flockhart staged an impressive recovery drive to finish fourth.

If the engine noise of the BRMs had always Impressed, the newer BRM now sported stub exhausts making its progress even more of an experience for those of us privileged to have seen these amazing cars in action.

The principal event of this Easter Monday meeting was the 21 lap Richmond Formule Libre race for the Glover Trophy, giving the BRMs another run, the two drivers swapping over to give Flockhart the newer car this time. Otherwise, the front row was as for the earlier Chichester Cup except that Rolt's Connaught had been repaired and was in its rightful place.

What should have been the highlight of the meeting, the race did not live up to its promise with several non-starters including '52/'53 Champion Alberto Ascari, prevented from appearing due to his Lancia contract. This was the race in which Wharton and Salvadori collided, the BRM continuing to win. It was so badly damaged as to be deemed beyond repair – perhaps the first time that a race was won by a 'write off'.

Enjoying a chat on the grid, Lance Macklin, works driver for the HWM Formula Two team, and Earl Howe.

Whoops!

Not everyone cleared the chicane unscathed. Over enthusiastic application of right foot to pedal as exemplified by John Keeling in the ex Ecosse C-type Jaguar **(right)** and **(below)**, Bert Rogers in 'TPD 1', known famously as 'Mucky Pup', a Bristol engined sports car originally built up on a Mk. 1 Cooper T20 frame by Tony Crook.

Bert Rogers ran the Sun-Pat peanut company and was to crash a Tojeiro fatally at Goodwood, Easter 1956.

I was to catch him in another spin at the Crystal Palace later in the year – was it something to do with me and my camera?

One example of the multitude of motor-cycle engined 500cc F3 cars, the Arengo was to be no competition for the Coopers and Kiefts. When first announced by its maker, Bristol based Clive Arengo, (**below**, with his wife), it sounded promising with a projected better power to weight ratio than its rivals and in the hands of Joe Fry of 'Freikaiserwagen' fame, the first version did win its first race, but against poor opposition. Note the Riley parked in the shade in this evocative paddock shot.

My older brother Gordon had settled in the Bristol area and for a time was involved with Arengo, building this car and acting as his racing mechanic. At this Goodwood meeting, Arengo's race ended on the first lap when Nuckey spun, taking the Arengo and Elliott's Cooper off with him. (top right), Clive Arengo, with my brother, examine the damage.

The race was won by Reg Bicknell (Revis) and a certain Ken Tyrell, later to achieve distinction as a World Championship winning constructor and team owner, came home third in a Cooper.

My brother scrambling his Triumph Tiger 100 somewhere in Sussex in the early '50s, watched with interest and perhaps apprehension by our parents.

Peter Collins

In 1954, Peter Collins was still some way from becoming a star Grand Prix driver – that was to begin two years later, driving for Ferrari. As with Stirling Moss, his close contemporary, he began in 500cc racing, moving to the F2 HWM team through '52-'53 combining a successful sports car career with the Aston Martin team, winning the 1952 Goodwood Nine Hours and the '53 Tourist Trophy, both times partnered by Pat Griffith.

Tony Vandervell took notice of his rising career and gave him this opportunity behind the wheel of his 'Thin Wall Special' to win the Whitsun Trophy, beating the BRM of Ron Flockhart and Salvadori's Maserati 250F. This led on to his drives with the embryo Vanwall as the Vandervell organisation worked towards later Grand Prix success. In the 1955 Targa Florio, he shared the winning Mercedes-Benz 300SLR with Moss. 1956 found him not only with a Ferrari drive but teamed with no less than Juan Manuel Fangio.

Staying with Ferrari through the next two years, now teamed with Mike Hawthorn, he was to lose his life at the Nurburgring in 1958. It is a sad irony that he was chasing hard after the Vanwall of Tony Brooks. Enzo Ferrari himself was deeply affected by his death, having a very high opinion of this young, handsome and charming man.

Ron Flockhart

Ron Flockhart, who went on to win Le Mans twice, first in 1956 with Ninian Sanderson in an Ecurie Ecosse Jaguar and again in 1957 with Ivor Bueb, here, was new to the BRM team. He was, however, to play a loyal and important role in the marque's troubled development.

On the grid for the Chichester Cup race **(below)**, with BRM press officer Rivers-Fletcher, **(below right)** what the well dressed racing driver was wearing that year and **(right)** in the original Mk.1 car, chassis no. 1/02.

As well as motor racing, Flockhart had a fascination for aviation and he was to die while practising for an event in Australia in a World War II P51 Mustang fighter in 1962, the very year that BRM won both the Constructor's and driver's F1 titles. It was sad that the driver who had done so much to take the team forward was no longer around to witness their success.

Sporting much cleaner lines than the Mk I, it seems amazing that so much effort was still being devoted to developing this car, after the GP formula had moved on, restricting it to formule libre for the past two years.

Ken Wharton (**above right**) *and Ron Flockhart* (**right**) *sampling the sleeker short chassis Mk II P30 BRM during one of the practice sessions for the Whitsun meeting.*

BRITISH GRAND PRIX, SILVERSTONE, JULY 1954

Coming from their impressive return to the Grand Prix scene just two weeks earlier after their debut win in the French GP at Reims, this marked the first appearance of Mercedes-Benz on British soil since coming to Donington before the war in 1937/38. As before and very much in charge, their formidable and imposing team manager Alfred Neubauer **(right)**.

Legendary for his management of the 'Silver Arrows' in the days of Caracciola, von Brauchitsch, Lang and Seaman, his experience set him in a class apart and his team was once again set to dominate over the next two years. But it was not to be here at Silverstone, the all enveloping streamlined bodies which had worked so well in France proved not to be so suitable on the airfield circuit.

I joined an interested crowd as we gathered round to get our first sight of the German cars' arrival in the paddock – Kling's Mercedes is eased out of its transporter and an anxious mechanic checks the nose for ground clearance.

Left open in the paddock for all to see, the straight eight-cylinder two and half litre Mercedes engine was technically advanced in every respect, sporting fuel injection and desmodromic valve gear and to reduce the car's height, the designers had tilted it over through 70 degrees. Mercedes were not yet convinced about disc brakes however, fitting large drum brakes, mounted inboard to reduce unsprung weight, those for the front wheels clearly visible in this shot.

The view over the cockpit (**below left**) perhaps gives some idea of the difficulty experienced by the drivers in placing their front wheels for the corners, not a problem at Reims with its open bends but with sand filled oil drums lining Silverstone's corners, definitely an issue.

Thorough as always, the German team was well known for fabricating new parts overnight in response to a driver's needs and they had come to Silverstone well prepared with a fully equipped workshop truck and another full of spares.

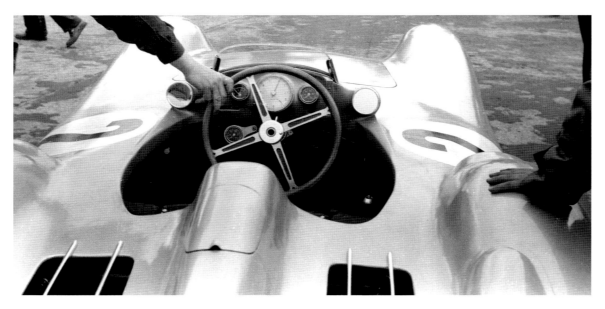

The two Mercedes-Benz W196 Stromlinienwagen cars (**right**) for Fangio and Kling receive attention behind the pits. Fangio is back to camera at the left, taking a close interest in the preparation of his car.

The pits in those days were little more than the length of a car deep, so there was too little room to work on the cars under cover, unlike the clean and spacious 'laboratories' of today. I took this shot from the pits roof – it shows well the large plan area of these 'streamliners', in contrast to their low build.

A cheerful Karl Kling (**above**) splashes his way past the pits following a shower during practice. He had good reason to be happy – two weeks earlier at Reims, he had finished second to Fangio in the Mercedes one-two in his first Grand Prix at the age of 44. He was an amateur driver before the war and this drive was reward for the months of testing and development work he had put in to help bring about the re-birth of Daimler-Benz as a force in post war motor racing.

I found the inside of Chapel Curve a good place to shoot during practice sessions, bearing in mind my lack of a photographers pass – there was just nobody near to question my presence. Crouching low as Kling drifts by into Hangar Straight, the view shows off the low lines of the W196.

Fangio with Reg Parnell, one-off team mates with Alfa Romeo in that very first F1 GP at Silverstone in 1950

Joining the Mercedes-Benz team in '54 was to give Fangio his second and third World Championships. He qualified on pole, but not without making a supreme effort, the Ferraris of Gonzalez and Hawthorn a second slower and Moss, Maserati close behind to complete the front row. Grids were set then by best laps during practice sessions, no special qualifying session. Fangio's time, with this two and a half litre car beat both Farina's outright lap record with the 'Thin Wall' as well as that of Gonzalez in the '51 GP, both with their two extra litres, such was progress.

Jose Froilan Gonzalez – 'Pepe' or 'The Pampas Bull' – the other Argentinian. Always perhaps, a little overshadowed by his compatriot Fangio, he was nevertheless, one of the great drivers of the period. Invited by Fangio to join the Equipo Argentino for 1950, he regarded 1954 'my best year – I won a lot of races'. Amongst them Le Mans, driving for Ferrari with Maurice Trintignant and here at Silverstone for the second time.

I was lucky to have seen all three of the the British Grand Prix Gonzalez drove in, his victory in 1951 being especially memorable – the first time the hitherto all conquering Alfa Romeos had been beaten as well as being the first Formula One GP victory for the Ferrari team. This time, he would line up second only to Fangio on the grid.

After his time with Gordini, Maurice Trintignant (**above**), now had a works Ferrari drive, joining Gonzalez and Mike Hawthorn (**right**) – a deserved recognition of his talent. He qualified on the third row.

For the second year running, Mike Hawthorn wound up third on the grid. Note the goggles and cravat, not his usual visor and bow tie.

Lined up in the paddock, three of the Maserati entries. Nearest, the A6GCM of Mieres, then 250Fs for Onofre Marimon and Villoresi. Lancia had agreed to release Ascari and Villoresi to support Marimon for this race, their cars not yet ready but while the drivers were present, the two Fiat lorries with the cars had gone to the wrong port and only arrived at midday on the Friday. A special practice session was arranged but it meant Ascari and Villoresi were relegated to the back of the grid – all very Italian!

Eclipsed by Ferrari and Mercedes, Maserati recognised the skills of Stirling Moss **(right)**. The factory would maintain his engine and Moss could forget his previous rev limit. He gained a fine fourth place to sit on the outside of the front row of the grid.

The Gordini team deserves much credit for its persistence over many years and fielded three cars for Jean Behra, Andre Pilette and Clemar Bucci. Behra, impressive in practice, found himself on the second row alongside Karl Kling in the second Merc.

Below: *Behra perhaps undertaking team leader duties, shows Bucci the way round. He lined up on the fourth row with team-mate Pilette.*

Above: *Among the supporting cast, Peter Whitehead in the Cooper Alta makes room for the Vanwall Special driven by Peter Collins, motoring through on a faster lap. The Vanwall had a chassis based on Ferrari lines, but built by Coopers and started with an F2 2 litre engine, enlarged here to 2.3 litres. When it first appeared, it had an ugly surface tube radiator, now shrouded over, which at least made things easier to paint its Number 20!*

Right: *While Tony Vandervell continued his efforts to build a winning British GP car, rivals BRM financed by Alfred Owen, had bought a 250F Maserati to gain experience while developing their own car. Ken Wharton put it on the third row.*

Continuing to help me reach parts of Silverstone for which I had no pass, Rob Walker's team from Dorking wheel their Connaught to the grid. This season, the Walker car was driven by Riseley-Prichard who skidded out 10 laps from the finish.

Standing by no. 26 **(right)** the Ecurie Ecosse entered Connaught, is Leslie Thorne. These drivers, qualifying well down on the grid, had the unusual experience of lining up ahead of World Champion Ascari and his Maserati team mates.

Throughout the weekend, whenever Fangio came within range of my camera, I always seemed to catch him looking decidedly unhappy, whether sitting on an oil drum (labelled 'Silvertown'!) or chatting to Mercedes engineers. Perhaps he was contemplating the difficult task ahead, steering the streamlined, wide-bodied car safely past all the oil drums lining the corners, shown clearly in this shot of him negotiating Beckets. He still managed to put it on pole, though. Note the lone marshall in charge of the Maggots, Beckets and Chapel series of corners.

Number One Mercedes sits quietly on pole, waiting for maestro Fangio to conduct it through 90 laps of the Grand Prix. The characters around it repay study – no last minute panics for the German trio on the left, the photographer lines up his Rollei, two senior firemen take an interest and a Boy Scout somehow has an 'official' armband.

Drivers were given a briefing on the grid before lining up. Bob Gerard, nearest, left, Stirling Moss and Roy Salvadori in the middle and Mike Hawthorn, pursing his lips, among them.

Right: Works Maserati driver Onofre Marimon, fellow countryman and protegee of Fangio, walks to his car while Ascari calls for attention.

Far right: Gonzalez and his Ferrari team manager look as though they already have the race won!

MIXED FORTUNES
While Hawthorn prepares to take his front row position (right), World Champion Ascari walks down to the other end of the grid.

One minute to go and the signal is given to fire up the engine of Fangio's car while Hawthorn checks his watch **(left)**. Between them Gonzalez, perhaps thinking back to 1951 when he also sat next to race favourite Fangio on the grid in, it seemed, a superior car. Could he come out on top again?

The flag drops and the second row of the seventh RAC British Grand Prix accelerates away **(above)** with Salvadori's Maserati edging ahead of Kling's W196 and Behra's Gordini. The Vanwall, with its strange nose and odd radiator is just moving from its third row slot.

The race had started on a dry track but with rain threatening. Gonzalez went straight into the lead and soon had a five second advantage over Fangio with Hawthorn, Moss, Behra and Marimon next up. Evidence of just how hard Fangio was trying to stay with Gonzalez soon showed – the nose on both sides bearing witness to close contact with those oil drum corner markers.

At one third distance, pit signals told Gonzalez the gap to Fangio was still 5 seconds.

Above: *Ascari – during practice – soon ran into trouble in the race, retiring his Maserati with valve trouble.*

Above right: *Villoresi was quickly pulled in and Ascari took over, only to to break down later, 'loss of oil' being given as the reason. Maserati's 250F was demonstrating its speed but work was needed on reliability and team organisation.*

Right: *Karl Kling had a difficult time in the second Mercedes, having a nasty moment at Copse as the track became slippery with rain and found himself following Ascari, now in Villoresi's car.*

Behind the two leaders, a great duel developed between Moss and Hawthorn, each taking it in turns to lead the other. As light rain began to dampen the track, Moss closed up to and then took Fangio to move into second place, Hawthorn soon also following through. Apart from the difficulty Fangio was having lining his car up for the corners, his gear lever was having to be held in fourth to prevent it jumping out.

After the French GP, it had been expected that the German team would also dominate this race but it was not working out that way at all.

At last, Moss had a car worthy of his talent and no longer tied to second division British cars, was making the most of it, putting on a real virtuoso display. While Gonzalez continued to lead, the exciting duel behind between the two home drivers finally resolved itself in Moss's favour, the patriotic crowd revelling in the situation.

Onofre Marimon (33) laps the Connaught of Leslie Thorne (26) on his way to a fine third place, giving Maserati some joy after the tribulations experienced by Ascari and Villoresi.

An enormously promising and popular young driver, Marimon was to lose his life just two months later at the Nurburgring while practising for the German Grand Prix.

Bira shared the third row on the grid with Collins, Wharton and Trintignant in his 250F Maserati **(below)** but was taken ill and handed over to Ron Flockhart who promptly crashed it comprehensively on lap 44, flipping over three times.

As Flockhart was driving at the behest of BRM, they put all Bira's surviving bits on the Owen chassis and effectively gave Bira their car in compensation.

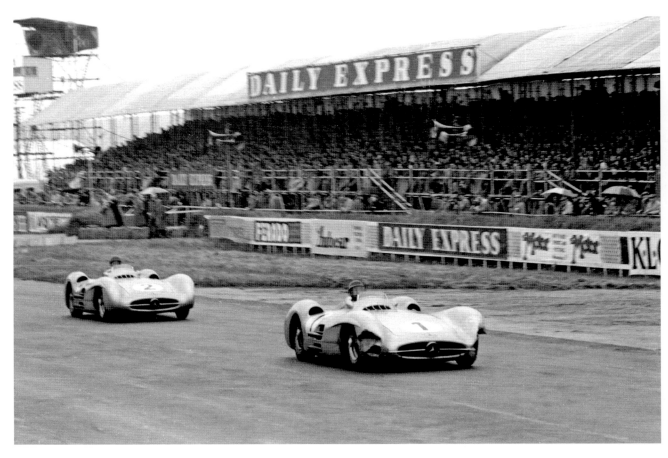

On their debut in the French Grand Prix, Fangio and Kling did indeed run together, finishing in a famous one-two. Here at Silverstone, Fangio, his car showing its battle scars, has lapped his team mate and is running to a fourth place finish while Kling will finish seventh, 3 laps down.

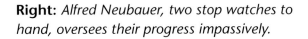

Right: *Alfred Neubauer, two stop watches to hand, oversees their progress impassively.*

While Moss's mechanic Alf Francis signals, the 'management' in the Maserati pit makes quite a study as the race runs towards the finish.

Alas, it was not to be for Moss, his back axle failing just 10 laps from the end. As Tony Robinson and Alf Francis push the car away, Bernard Cahier, with Leica camera, commiserates with a hugely disappointed Moss.

As I raised my own Leica to take this shot of Stirling walking away, my feelings at seeing such a fine run come to this sad end were shared all round the track.

Watched by his team manager, pit signals have little to tell Gonzalez – how many laps to go and an unchanged race position. Ferrari came from Reims to Silverstone out for revenge and Gonzalez duly delivered – a classic non-stop drive in the lead all the way to win the British Grand Prix for the second time.

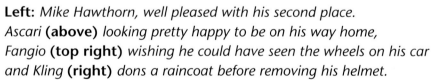

Left: *Mike Hawthorn, well pleased with his second place.*
Ascari (**above**) *looking pretty happy to be on his way home,*
Fangio (**top right**) *wishing he could have seen the wheels on his car*
and Kling (**right**) *dons a raincoat before removing his helmet.*

Drivers sprint to their cars at the start of the big sports car race which followed the Grand Prix on an almost dry course. Nearest, no. 30, the HWM of George Abecassis and 35, Ninian Sanderson's Ecurie Ecosse C-type Jaguar. DB3S Aston Martins had a clean sweep, Peter Collins leading Roy Salvadori and American Caroll Shelby home.

Above: *Reg Parnell reaches for the starter of his Lagonda..*

Right: *Parnell , number 41, has winner Peter Collins' DB3S (20) to his left and Peter Walker's C-type (34) just ahead. Parnell came in fourth, behind the Astons.*

Above right: *Further down the field, the Mk2 Mille Miglia Frazer-Nash of Peter Reece and a trio of C-types.*

CRYSTAL PALACE AUGUST MEETING

The main race at the August meeting was the appropriately named August Trophy, to be run in two heats and a final. **(Below right)** Reg Parnell won the first heat in his Ferrari from Salvadori's Maserati. Here he is followed by Horace Gould (Cooper Bristol) and Paul Emery (Emeryson). **(Below)** Rolt closes on Jack Fairman in the unique Turner formula two car, on his way to victory in the second heat. In the final, Parnell won from Salvadori's Maserati and Rolt.

Right: *Not for nothing was burly Horace Gould nicknamed 'The Gonzalez of the West Country'. A dream subject for this budding photographer, lap after lap, he drifted his agile car through the corners in this most exuberant fashion.*

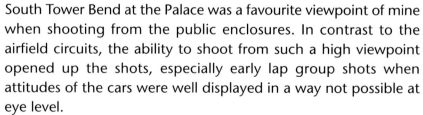

South Tower Bend at the Palace was a favourite viewpoint of mine when shooting from the public enclosures. In contrast to the airfield circuits, the ability to shoot from such a high viewpoint opened up the shots, especially early lap group shots when attitudes of the cars were well displayed in a way not possible at eye level.

Left: *Lap 1 of the sports car race and Tony Crook in the sports Cooper Bristol leads Cliff Davis's Tojeiro Bristol, Bert Rogers (Cooper Bristol) and Roy Salvadori in the A6GCS sports Maserati.*

Above: *On lap 2, Salvadori has passed Rogers and will soon pass Davis, only to crash while attempting to catch the leader. Fourth in this picture is Tony Brooks driving Hely's Frazer Nash who came through to finish second behind Crook with Rogers third.*

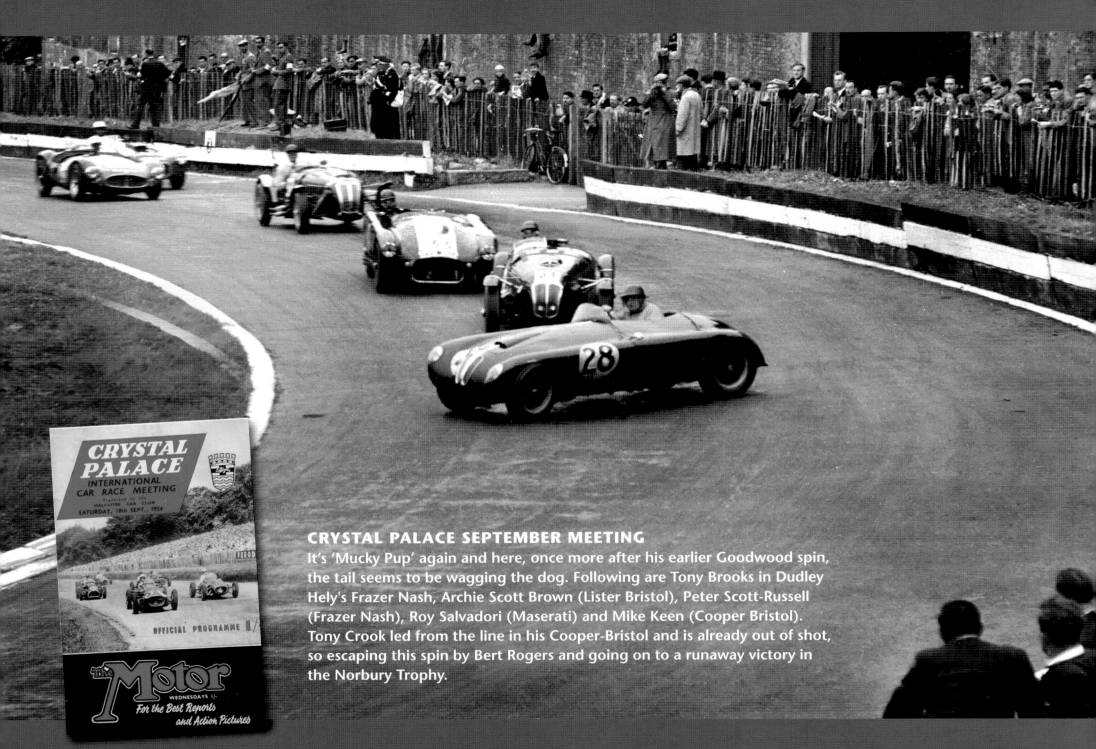

CRYSTAL PALACE SEPTEMBER MEETING

It's 'Mucky Pup' again and here, once more after his earlier Goodwood spin, the tail seems to be wagging the dog. Following are Tony Brooks in Dudley Hely's Frazer Nash, Archie Scott Brown (Lister Bristol), Peter Scott-Russell (Frazer Nash), Roy Salvadori (Maserati) and Mike Keen (Cooper Bristol). Tony Crook led from the line in his Cooper-Bristol and is already out of shot, so escaping this spin by Bert Rogers and going on to a runaway victory in the Norbury Trophy.

CRYSTAL PALACE INTERNATIONAL CAR RACE MEETING Organised by the HALF-LITRE CAR CLUB SATURDAY, 18th SEPT., 1954

OFFICIAL PROGRAMME 1/-

The Motor WEDNESDAYS 1/- For the Best Reports and Action Pictures

GOODWOOD, SEPTEMBER 25TH 1954

Rounding out the 1954 season, Goodwood's International Meeting in September and the 21 lap Goodwood Trophy race for F1 cars gets under way. Moss, far side on pole led throughout, but as an indication of the progress British GP cars were making, Peter Collins in the no. 8 'Vanwall Special' held on to a creditable second place. Next in line, Bob Gerard's Cooper Bristol and Reg Parnell's Ferrari is nearest camera.

Attitude of car and driver says speed. Stirling Moss takes the left-hander at St. Mary's in style while showing off the classic lines of this iconic '50s GP car, the Maserati 250F. Just visible above the exhaust pipe is a golden eagle, mast head of the 'Eagle' comic for boys. Of course, advertising was not allowed!

Before the Goodwood Trophy race, Moss had placed second in two events, the 500cc race and the up to 2 litre sports car race and no doubt wanted to make sure of this win as his entry was now by the official Maserati team.

Foreign entries in this 'international' meeting were few and far between but French veteran driver Louis Rosier **(left)** did come over to compete in his 250F Maserati, finishing eighth in the Goodwood Trophy. Reg Parnell's Ferrari, no doubt tired after its exertions throughout the year, retired on the third lap, disappointing after his successes at the earlier Goodwood meetings.

Tony Vandervell's 'Vanwall Special' **(right)** had a chassis built by Coopers, an engine developed from Norton motor cycle technology and, with additional input from Colin Chapman and Frank Costin, would later put Britain at the front of Grands Prix. In the race Peter Collins obviously got too close to something on his way to second place!

I make no apology for including one more picture of the 'Thin Wall Special' in the swansong days of formule libre racing. 'Formule Libre' was born out of the FIA decision to run the whole 1952 World Championship to Formula Two following the withdrawal of Alfa Romeo – to continue with the existing formula would have left Ferrari with mainly outdated opposition. In Britain, this left the V16 BRMs high and dry, but with Tony Vandervell steadily working on his own plans for a future British GP contender with his Ferrari based 'Thin Wall Special', race organisers saw an opportunity, with the resulting races providing some glorious spectacle as well as memorable sounds over two or three more years.

A good entry in the unlimited sports car race produced some close racing.

At the time, I no doubt felt envious of the official photographers silhouetted on their raised platform but I like the atmosphere of these against the light shots.

Left: *Jack Fairman leads this group in an HWM Jaguar from Michael Head's C-type Jaguar with Bert Rogers in the 'Mucky Pup' Cooper Bristol bringing up the rear.*

Below left: *Mike Hawthorn leads, driving a 3 litre Monza Ferrari entered by Joe Kelly with George Abecassis, HWM Jaguar and Tony Brooks' Frazer Nash Le Mans Replica following. Abecassis finished third behind Masten Gregory's Ferrari and winner Roy Salvadori in the Ecurie Ecosse C-type. Hawthorn's Ferrari retired with a failed back axle.*

In the sports car race for cars up to two litres Roy Salvadori had his second sports car victory of the day, driving the Sydney Greene Maserati A6GCS. Here he leads Stirling Moss driving the Lister-Bristol which should have had Archie Scott-Brown at the wheel. There had been some query over his competition licence due to his disabilities and it had been temporarily withdrawn, thankfully quickly reinstated.

National Service and into the real world

Luck was to be with me on leaving school in 1950. My entry into the RAF for my National Service was delayed until the start of 1951, so keen was I to get into photography that I had investigated signing up for an extra year. In the end, I was told that I could sign my life away but photography was closed. Then, although I had been in the Air Training Corps at school and should therefore have only served six weeks 'square bashing', this was somehow overlooked and I did the full eight weeks. When I got my posting, it was to the RAF School of Photography

at Wellesbourne Mountford and I was in the very first intake when photography opened up again. Without those delays, I think I was destined to be a radar mechanic.

Until demob early in 1953, my time was spent at RAF Benson with its aerial survey processing unit down the road at Ewelme. As one of the few 'erks' with a driving licence, I soon found myself driving the unit van and apart from collecting the odd film from the Mosquitos, my main duties when not processing and printing were to be collecting the tea and coffee urns as well as handling the doughnut order from the excellent cottage bakery in Ewelme village. Soon I was transferred to the night shift which started at 6.0pm and in theory could go on all night but almost never did. Nearly always in bed by midnight, excused morning parades and a late breakfast in the mess seemed pretty civilised to me as were Summer afternoons rowing on the Thames by Wallingford Bridge.

Starting out in the real world, I first worked at a local high street photographers in Redhill, involved in everything, commercial photography and weddings to developing customers' black and white films. One day, Donald Campbell came in with a rush order and I delivered the prints later in the evening to his home. Little did I know that our paths would cross again in a much more significant way in just over three

Two of my early industrial shots from the Monotype days, (left) coating a litho plate and (right) making a master letter for a Monotype font.

years time. Later that year, I was approached by the Monotype Corporation at Salfords leading to a job in their R & D department where they were developing a photographic typesetting version of their hot metal type composing machine. Over the next eighteen months, while not involved in the creative industrial photography I hoped to progress to, I learned much about photographic technique and quality control. The master negatives for the machine, holding 256 characters on a 5' x 4' glass plate had to be produced to the most exacting standards. When the company's staff photographer moved on in 1955, I took his place and the foundations of my career in industrial and commercial photography fell into place.

Gradually, while my interest in motor racing continued, recording it with my camera became a lower priority for me. The negatives were put on one side, gradually to be forgotten and not resurrected for fifty years.

My life was moving in other directions.

GOODWOOD

BRITISH AUTOMOBILE RACING CLUB
INTERNATIONAL MOTOR RACING
MONDAY 11th APRIL 1955
FIRST RACE 1·30 PM

Official Souvenir Programme   2 s

The Autocar

EVERY
FRIDAY

always first in the field   1/-

THE EASTER GOODWOOD MEETING saw Peter Collins still driving in 'Formule Libre' but now in the BRM, and with the 'Thin Wall' in retirement, the main opposition came from the 250F Maseratis of Roy Salvadori and Stirling Moss, finishing in that order behind the well driven BRM in the Chichester Cup.

Having said goodbye to the 'Thin Wall Special' at the end of last year, this was to be the last time I would hear the glorious sounds of that V16 BRM engine in full flight *(above)*. Never to be forgotten.

1955

Michael Poberejsky, who raced under the pseudonym of Mike Sparken, handled his Ferrari 3-litre impeccably and appeared to have the over 3-litre sports car race in his pocket, leading all the way from Duncan Hamilton's Jaguar D-type and Salvadori's Aston Martin. But both Sparken and Hamilton were given a 15 second penalty for jumped starts, handing the win to Salvadori.

It was Salvadori's day as he also won both the Lavant Cup and the Richmond F1 Glover Trophy, first in a Connaught and then a 250F Maserati. In each race, he was chased home by Bob Gerard's Cooper Bristol (16) and the Connaught of Don Beauman (5)

The Stirling Moss Maserati was decidedly off colour at this meeting. Newly fitted with disc brakes and SU fuel injection, more development was clearly needed but this was the year when Moss would move on to drive for Mercedes-Benz, winning the British GP at Aintree and his famous drive to triumph in the Mille Miglia.

Right: *A new B-type Connaught appeared with all-enveloping body and tail fin, Tony Rolt at the wheel. Difficult to handle and uncompetitive, it was soon abandoned.*

The new 'Bobtail' Cooper Climax T39 would spawn the F2 and then the F1 Cooper which would change the face of motor racing. Here Tommy Sopwith leads Ivor Bueb.

CRYSTAL PALACE
International Car Race Meeting
ORGANIZED BY THE
BRITISH AUTOMOBILE RACING CLUB
SATURDAY 30th JULY 1955
OFFICIAL PROGRAMME
1/-

The Motor
WEDNESDAYS 1/-
For the Best Reports and Action Pictures

Colin Chapman was a fine driver as well as a constructor of the Lotus cars. He won the 2 litre sports car race ahead of Ivor Bueb and Tommy Sopwith in Coopers.

Cooper provided a chassis into which the Gilby Engineering Co put a 2 litre Maserati engine. Driven here by Roy Salvadori, the car is followed by John Rolls in the ex-Cliff Davis Tojeiro Bristol and John Coombs in Lotus Connaught Mk. IX.

In a gesture that seems remarkable today, Stirling Moss lent his Maserati 250F to rival Mike Hawthorn who thanked him by winning the main race of the day. Moss was now a works Mercedes driver but that was no excuse for painting the Maserati pale grey.

Horace Gould drove the third Maserati 250F in the race. The picture typifies the West Countryman's 'press on' style.

Tony Vandervell's Vanwall Special had been modified from the prototype and the word 'Special' dropped from its title. It would be another year before Chapman and Costin would transform the car but in the meantime Harry Schell would do his best.

Hawthorn, Gould and Schell are followed by Paul Emery in the Emeryson and Salvadori in the other Maserati of the group.

SATURDAY, AUGUST 20th, 1955

GOODWOOD NINE-HOUR RACE

3 p.m. UNTIL MIDNIGHT

OFFICIAL PROGRAMME 2s

The Autocar

Best from start to finish - Fridays 1s

GOODWOOD, AUGUST 20TH 1955

Bringing a touch of Le Mans to West Sussex, the atmosphere builds as the cars are lined up for the start of the third Goodwood Nine Hour sports car race. The summer sun has brought out the hydrangeas, but not a large number of spectators.

The Aston Martin works team of DB3S cars line up at the start (l to r) for Walker/Poore, Collins/Brooks and Parnell/Salvadori. Aston Martin had been victorious in the previous two Goodwood Nine Hours races but faced stiff competition here with works 3-litre Ferrari 750 Monzas for Hawthorn/Portago, Schell/Lucas and Wharton/Jonneret as well as virtually works Jaguars and the lone Ecurie Ecosse D-type.

Above: *My friend Alan R Smith peers into his favourite camera, an Ikoflex twin lens reflex, spurning 35mm in favour of the larger 6x6cm negative.*

The drivers take up their positions opposite the cars.
Hawthorn (Ferrari), Walker (Aston Martin), Collins (Aston Martin),
Parnell (Aston Martin), Sanderson (Jaguar) and Jonneret (Ferrari)

To the right of Sanderson and Jonneret are Rolt (Jaguar), Schell (Ferrari), Macklin (HWM), Russell (Cooper), Moss (Porsche) Whitehead (Jaguar), Chapman (Lotus), Leston (Connaught), Berry (Jaguar), Sopwith (Cooper), Marsh (Cooper), Hampshire (Lister), Marshall (HWM), McAlpine (Connaught), Seidel (Porsche), Davis (Lotus), Keen (Cooper), Coombs (Lotus).

They're off and Hawthorn's long legs cover the ground the quickest. But the prize for most stylish sprinter must go to Rolt, far right.

The old control tower made a fine viewing point for me to shoot this sequence of the Le Mans start.

The middle of the pack sets off with Colin Chapman's Lotus IX dodging ahead of the almost stalled Stirling Moss Porsche (34), while Peter Whitehead's Jaguar D, Bob Berry's sister car, Tony Marsh in Bradnack's Cooper Jaguar, John Marshall's HWM Jaguar, and David Hampshire's Lister Bristol form a polite queue to work round the obstruction. Hanging fire is the Bristol powered Cooper T39 (23) which was later to crash, taking the life of Mike Keen.

Moss has got his Porsche straightened up but the engine is still not firing properly, causing confusion all round. The Rolls brothers Tojeiro Bristol (26) gets clear but McAlpine's Connaught (30) finds itself completely blocked. Macklin in HWM Jaguar (14) has a clear run but Hampshire, Lister (22) and Coombs in Lotus 9 (38) get a little too close to the crowded pit lane.

In spite of his hesitant start, Stirling Moss **(left)** had the 1500cc Porsche Spyder in a respectable position when he handed over to Hushke von Hanstein. The car then slipped down the order until the master retook the wheel. He clawed his way back to a class lead and sixth overall only to be collected by the spinning Cooper-Bristol of Tony Crook with about two hours still to go, the resulting damage forcing retirement and the loss of a likely class win.

The Schell/Lucas car was the first of the three Ferraris to retire. Gearbox problems ended its run after 184 laps.

The Ecurie Ecosse D Type Jaguar (11) of Desmond Titterington and Ninian Sanderson in close company with the similar car of Rolt/Hamilton. Tony Rolt would retire after only 13 laps with a sheared distributor drive.

Despite the attention of works mechanics, the Ferrari pit stops owed more to Italian comic opera. Only side jacks were used, causing the cars to block the pit road during the resulting lengthy stops as they were backed in diagonally to the pit counter.

Mike Hawthorn in the Ferrari 750 Monza with which he led the race, aided by co-driver the Marquis de Portago. Although nominally private entries, all three Monzas had full Ferrari works support and this was the second one to retire at 219 laps.

Above: *The arrow points the way as a Lotus heads down towards St Mary's.*

Left: *The Jonneret/Wharton Ferrari lasted the longest of the three – 229 laps, before retiring with 'oil leaks' given as the reason.*

Looking across the concrete barrier toward the corn stooks, both Goodwood
trade marks, the Hampshire/Scott Russell Lister Bristol leads the Ecurie Ecosse
Jaguar and a Cooper in the evening light at Fordwater.

The burned out, overturned wreckage of Mike Keen's Cooper Bristol lies amongst the corn stooks at Fordwater, witness to a tragic accident. Before the race was two hours old, the driver sustained head injuries in the accident from which he later died in hospital.

Below: The Ecurie Ecosse D-Type Jaguar of Desmond Titterington and Ninian Sanderson, with the South Downs behind, speeding on its way to second place.

Dennis Poore in the winning Aston Martin DB3S, the result giving the Feltham concern a clean sweep of the classic nine hour races.

Still three hours to go and dusk turns to night. The atmosphere builds and speeding cars leave light traces from their headlamps.

1956

Variety Club

Three into one won't go! A typical mix of machinery at a Goodwood Members' Meeting – **(left)** the Allard J2X of David Lewis leads Peter Blond's C-type Jaguar and the HWM of George Abecassis as they brake for the chicane.

At the same club meeting **(above)** a Cooper Jaguar driven by Michael Head leads the Abecassis HWM Jaguar.

Right, top to bottom: *the 300SL Mercedes Benz of Tony Everard, Mort Morris Goodall's Aston Martin DB3S and the Riley RM of George Grace.*

INTERNATIONAL TROPHY, SILVERSTONE, MAY 1956

A sign of changing times – British cars with real prospects of success at last. Lined up in front of the pits before practising for the Daily Express International Trophy race, one of the new Vanwalls and two of the five works 'Syracuse' Connaughts beyond.

Following Connaught's sensational win late last season at the Syracuse GP, Tony Brooks at the wheel, I joined a patriotic British crowd gathered at Silverstone hoping for more of the same and was not to be disappointed.

G A Vandervell had entered two of the new Vanwalls for Stirling Moss and Harry Schell. Quite different in appearance to last year's prototype, with new aerodynamic bodies designed by Mike Costin over space frames, the work of Colin Chapman, hopes were high for both drivers as their qualifying times were a second faster than Fangio in the Lancia Ferrari.

Left: *Moss accelerates past the hangar onto Hangar Straight.*

Seriously underfunded, Connaught nevertheless put up an impressive show with mechanics busy in the pits preparing the works cars to be driven by Archie Scott-Brown, Desmond Titterington, Jack Fairman, Mike Oliver and one, painted red in his honour, for Italian driver Piero Scotti.

Used to seeing several Ferraris or Maseratis lined up in the paddock, I must nevertheless have been impressed by all this activity by one of the home teams, judging by the number of frames I exposed on them!

Mike Hawthorn

After driving for both Vanwall and Ferrari the previous year, Mike Hawthorn signed up with BRM for the 1956 season. The team entered just one car for this event with Hawthorn showing its potential in qualifying to line up on the front row of the grid in fourth place.

Well known for usually wearing a bow tie when racing, I caught Mike here with more conventional neckwear!

Jack Fairman

I always took a keen interest in Jack Fairman's exploits on the tracks. As a boy brought up in Horley, I was familiar with Fairman's Garage, owned in fact by Jack's brother Geoff. My father had his car serviced there, my brother was apprenticed there and every now and then in the late '40s, I would get a glimpse of Jack's Type 35 Bugatti and other cars which he kept there.

The garage is now a Wetherspoons pub named 'The Jack Fairman'. He also once came to my school, which he had also attended, to give us a talk about his many racing experiences. I remember one occasion, waking up on a Sunday morning to the distant sound of the Bugatti going up and down through the gears out on the old Gatwick airfield.

Right: *Fairman shows off the clean lines of the 'Syracuse' Connaught.*

Among the supporting cast, Bob Gerard with his Cooper Bristol **(right)**, Rob Walker's newer B-type Connaught, this time driven by Reg Parnell **(below)** and Piotti's Maserati 250F **(below right)** seen here during practice but a non-starter in the race.

After several years steady development of the six-cylinder cars, Gordini introduced this new all enveloping eight cylinder T32 model late in '55 and one was entered for Andre Pilette to drive in the International Trophy race from which it retired with a broken back axle. Only two were built and proved to be uncompetitive. The marque, seriously underfunded, struggled on into early 1957 and then closed down.

The Pilettes were something of a motor racing dynasty, Andre Pilette's father having raced at Indianapolis in 1912 and Andre's son, Teddy, was a Formula 5000 racer in the '70s.

The main opposition to the British cars came in the shape of two Lancia-Ferrari D50s for Fangio (**above and opposite page**) and Peter Collins (**top**). Sophisticated radiator blanking – wired on corrugated cardboard – was employed to combat the cool weather during practice.

Above: *The V8 engine with its double choke down-draught carburettors was mounted at an angle to the centre line of the car.*

Before the big event, two sports car races

In the up to 1500cc Sports Car Race, Roy Salvadori (left) took a fine win in this Cooper-Climax from the Lotus-Climax of Colin Chapman (below right) who might well have given Roy a harder time had he not spun, dropping to fourth before recovering.

The attractive Maserati of Jo Bonnier (below left) was no match for the more agile Cooper and Lotus-Climaxes.

Right: *At the Le Mans start of the over 1500cc Sports Car Race, Desmond Titterington sprints to his D-type Jaguar.*

Below: *Ken Wharton (Ferrari, 28) and Alan Brown (Ecosse D-type Jaguar, 10) accelerate towards Copse followed by Mackay Fraser in the no. 31 Ferrari, the Aston Martin DB3S of Hans Davids (25) and Mike Youngs' Lotus 8 (below).*

Understeer . . .

This works Jaguar has been newly fitted with a de Dion back axle and will be driven in the race by Desmond Titterington but during practice, Mike Hawthorn took it out for a few laps, perhaps to check the handling.

. . . and oversteer

Stirling Moss in the Aston Martin DB3S with which he finished second to Salvadori's sister car.

Peter Whitehead, more usually seen driving Jaguars in sports car races, had this Maserati 300S for a change. Driving well, he was able to keep Mackay-Fraser's big Ferrari at bay.

Jack Fairman's works D-type Jaguar was fitted with Lucas fuel injection but retired from the race, a fate also waiting for him in the Trophy race when his Connaught was withdrawn before a bent valve wrecked the engine.

Top left: *Musy's Maserati 300S came third in the up to 3 litre class, beaten only by the Astons of Salvadori and Moss,*

Above: *Ken Wharton overtakes the Lister-Bristol of Allan Moore*

Left: *Archie Scott Brown in the Lister-Maserati won the 1500-2000cc class from two Lister-Bristols.*

Ninian Sanderson's Ecurie Ecosse Jaguar **(left)** and Reg Parnell's works Aston Martin **(below)** were two of the cars eliminated in a four car accident at Club Corner, which also took out Peter Collins in another works DB3S and Titterington's Jaguar.

The day belonged to Roy Salvadori as far as the sports car races were concerned, taking his second fine win with the works Aston Martin.

At the start of the International Trophy, Fangio from third place moves across in front of the two Vanwalls of Moss and Schell, Hawthorn almost keeping up with him.

My perch, as often before, was the pit counter of the Rob Walker team and all eyes there were searching for Parnell. Unfortunately, he was out at the first corner, gearbox problems.

Lap 1 and Hawthorn has taken the lead from Fangio, with Schell, Collins and Moss following.

Moss quickly moved up from fifth, taking first Collins and then team mate Schell **(left)** before hunting down Fangio **(below)**.

Over the next few laps, I noticed Hawthorn getting increasingly frustrated at the lack of pit signals from his team and next time round had my Leica ready to record his agitation.

Alas, it was not to last, the magneto drive shearing and bringing the car to a halt at Abbey Curve on lap 14. It had though, been a fine demonstration of the BRM's potential.

Fangio found himself in the unusual situation of chasing after one British car while trying to fend off another. By the time Hawthorn retired, Moss had taken the lead and by 20 laps, Fangio was nearly a minute behind.

Fangio played a little game with me here. I took this shot during a practice session out at Beckets, the slowest corner on the circuit back in the '50s. The apex to the bend is to my right and Fangio has set his car up under braking, all four wheels sliding as he moves over from the far side of the track. I have my knee resting against one of the oil drums lining the inside of the course but well away from the normal line. On one lap, he came right across to my side at full speed and disappeared down Hangar Straight. Next time round, I had moved well back to the infield and he came touring round, waving to me and grinning broadly.

There seemed to be no question about the pace of the BRM and Vanwall, both in their first race of the season, but there was still a question about reliability when Schell **(above)** joined Hawthorn on the retirement list. Would Moss' splendid run end the same way?

Peter Collins shows off the classic lines of the Lancia-Ferrari D50. After all his hard work earlier, helping to develop the Vanwall, he must have been wondering about his promotion to works Ferrari driver as he and Fangio chased after the clearly faster Vanwall of Moss.

Reliability concerns for the British cars may well have been justified but the next significant retirement was Fangio's, the D50's clutch giving up.

Collins (**opposite above**) was immediately pulled in to hand his car over to the master. Fangio (**right**) accelerates back into the fray in the Collin's number 2 car, only to retire again a few laps later, also with a broken clutch.

All these retirements brought Roy Salvadori's Maserati (**far right**) up into second place, in close company with Scott Brown's Connaught. The two had a tremendous duel, frequently swapping places until near the end of the race, Salvadori had a big accident, overturning at Stowe but fortunately without serious injury.

From the very beginning, Stirling Moss always hoped to achieve success in motor racing's top category with a British car. Here at last, after 180 miles of the Silverstone circuit he takes the chequered flag to win at a record speed of 100.47mph while sharing a new lap record of 102.30mph with Mike Hawthorn.

Not yet a victory in a World Championship F1 Grand Prix but a clear signal that British cars were becoming a force to be reckoned with.

A clearly delighted Archie Scott Brown **(above)** brought his Connaught through into second place with Desmond Titterington **(right)** third in the other surviving works Connaught. With Gerard's older Cooper Bristol fourth, the highest placed Continental car was the Gordini of da Silva Ramos in fifth.

While still at school, I had become a keen member of the Reigate Photographic Society and benefited greatly from the friendly criticism of my early photographic efforts but by 1956 my attendance had become quite infrequent. However, around the time of the 1956 Silverstone International Trophy meeting, another lucky break came my way at a meeting when another member mentioned 'neighbour of mine, works for an oil company, looking for a photographer – are you interested?'. The neighbour turned out to be the advertising manager of Mobil Oil Company and my job interview took place at his home where my motor racing pictures proved to be of interest. Mobil had held its first Mobil Economy Run in 1955 and I was asked to attend the finish and awards ceremony of the '56 event as a test and was soon offered the new position of Staff Photographer. It seemed that my racing photography had played a significant part in convincing my interviewer that if I could capture Moss at a hundred plus, I should be able to make a fair fist of shooting competitors in the Run at their more modest pace. What I had not been told was that they had another speed subject for me to work on, something rather faster than I had so far encountered on the tracks.

During my first morning in this new job, I was informed that I had just a few days to get ready to move up to the Lake District to join Donald Campbell and his 'Bluebird' team based in the Sun Hotel at Coniston where preparations were underway for an attempt by Campbell to raise his own World Water Speed Record which he had first set on Ullswater the year before. Some start to a new job! That first week flew by as I set about equipping myself, not an easy task when new cameras were like gold dust in those times of austerity. Instead of the desired Rolleiflex I had specified, I had to settle for the simpler Rolleicord and it was with this, my Leica and various developing paraphernalia that I travelled up to Coniston. At this time, my personal transport was a 200cc four-stroke Triumph Tiger Cub and it was suggested that it might be a good idea to have it with me as a runabout. It went with me on the train from Euston to Lancaster from where

Left: *This was early September and therefore the tail end of the holiday season, so there was much public interest as Bluebird was eased off its trailer and into the boathouse. Not all the spectators were holidaymakers however and unfortunately the boy up the tree was caught playing truant.*

A relaxed Donald Campbell enjoys a cigarette while waiting for Bluebird to be made ready.

Bluebird K7 arrives on its transporter against a background of the Yewdale Fells and it's a tricky manoeuvre to get through the gate on to the lane to the boathouse. Chief Mechanic Leo Villa watches for clearance while Project Manager Andrew Brown looks on. From pre-war days with Donald's father Sir Malcolm Campbell, the Graham Adams company of New Malden had transported the various Bluebirds to their record breaking venues.

I rode on up to Coniston. I already knew the Sun Hotel, having stayed there with my parents six years earlier, but this time the atmosphere was very different and suddenly I found myself thrown into a new world. Over the next two weeks I was to become not just acquainted with all the team members but to find myself very much included in the team. It was obvious that I would not be using my camera all the time and with many other jobs to be done, soon found myself helping to man the press office, putting out marker buoys and generally finding other excuses to mess about in boats.

Gradually, the tension built up as Bluebird was made ready and the press gathered in anticipation. As I took my photographs, I processed the films in my bedroom, using the hand basin and developing tanks which I loaded in the beer cellar after dark. To have prints made, I came to an arrangement with a photographer in Ambleside and this is where my Tiger Cub came in handy. By the end of two weeks, the journey time came down dramatically as I became familiar with every twist and turn of the Coniston to Ambleside road.

Far left: *A new, more streamlined moulded cockpit canopy was installed to replace the original squared off version. With Leo Villa and other team members, Campbell checks the fitting.*

Left: *As with Sir Malcolm, Leo Villa had a close working relationship with son Donald, guiding him through all the trials and tribulations encountered in record breaking attempts.*

Below left: *With Bluebird safely installed in the temporary boathouse, the refuelling installation on the jetty is checked out by one of the Mobil drivers on a nice break from normal duties.*

Below: *The 'Press Office', with Coniston Old Man behind. It had a telephone and a kettle, both vital to keeping the gentlemen of the press happy. Making hot drinks for all and sundry was just one of my extra curricula activities when not busy with my camera. The single telephone line was completely inadequate at newsworthy times when the gentlemen of the press would compete enthusiastically to be first in line or dash off to the call box in the village.*

With all the static preparations completed, time to fire up the Beryl engine and then take Bluebird out for a test run.

As part of the service we provided to the many press photographers waiting for some action was to take them out to the middle of the lake in a small launch to get close-ups. The sense of anticipation as we sat there waiting for Bluebird to accelerate towards us at between 150 and 200mph was something I shall never forget.

On 19 September 1956, Donald Campbell set a new World Water Speed Record of 225.6 mph in 'Bluebird' K7.

Right: He receives congratulations from Leo and the team.

There was quite a party in the Sun Hotel that evening and Connie Robinson had baked a special cake with the new record speed commemorated in an icing speedometer.

In those pre-Beeching days, Coniston still had its railway station almost next door to the Sun Hotel and the next morning I was on my way back south to reality and to properly begin my new job.

November 1957

Just over a year later, in October 1957, I was back again in Coniston. Earlier in the year, Bluebird had been shipped on board the 'United States' across the Atlantic for an attempt on Lake Canandaigua.
Adverse underwater currents there forced a move to Lake Onandago but again the conditions proved too difficult, prompting a move back to Coniston. The team were also still learning about the craft, in particular its tendency to ship water before getting up to planing speed. It was found that this had damaged some of the turbine blades, making an engine change necessary. As another sideline to my main duties, I went over to Barrow-in-Furness with one of the local Mobil representatives to hire a suitable crane which came over the next morning.

Clockwise: *With the Beryl engine installed, a static test at the jetty to ensure all systems were connected up correctly and then, with conditions looking promising, Bluebird was fuelled up for a test run.*

On 7 November 1957, we all gathered down by the boathouse before dawn to witness one of those magical Lake District winter mornings. Coniston Water was perfectly still, the opposite shore white with frost mirrored in the lake – perfect conditions for the record attempt. Connie Robinson delivered egg and bacon sandwiches while we waited for the sun to rise and then it was all action as Bluebird was made ready for its skipper.

Instead of going out into the middle
of the lake onboard the press launch, I decided
to stay on the jetty, wishing to record a different perspective
of the occasion on this very special morning. After what seemed an
age, we heard Bluebird speeding back, then the flurry of spray as she slowed to settle
in the water and drift back to the jetty, Campbell opened the canopy, eager to know
whether he had done enough. He had – another new record at 239.07 mph.

Well wrapped up against the cold, key members of the team once again share the pleasure of a new mark in the record books. In two years, Donald Campbell had set new records on no less than four occasions, first on Ullswater, then in the US on Lake Mead followed by these two on Coniston Water.

Donald Campbell was to go on raising the Water Speed record another four times with Bluebird K7 over the next ten years, setting it at 276.33 mph in 1964, the same year that he set a new World Land Speed Record for wheel driven cars at 403.10mph in his Bluebird CN7 – the only man to have taken both records in the same year.

Over the winter of 1966/67 he once more went to Coniston, hoping to exceed 300mph, leading to the well documented fatal accident on January 4th 1967. Now buried on the edge of the cemetery in Coniston, he is finally at home in the village which played such a part in the history of water speed record breaking, both for Donald and his father, Sir Malcolm.

Passport to industry

More than a year into my work at Mobil, I had found that the job was like a passport into virtually every industry, quite apart from the obvious oil company subjects and this at a time when Britain still had a significant industrial base. Mobil was especially strong in industrial and marine lubricants and so steelworks, ships and shipyards, light and heavy engineering as well as industries using oil derived chemical products all became subjects for my cameras.

Left and top:
Velindre steelworks, South Wales, 1957 and (**above**) *cutting oil flowing in a lathe making gear wheels for the motor industry.*

The skills I had been acquiring while photographing motor racing served me well when shooting this tanker coming up the Channel off Dungeness.

My camera platform was a Cessna 172 flying at right angles across the bow, making timing critical to place the tanker exactly in the sunlit path. All credit to my pilot who judged speed, height and path exactly to place me perfectly for my shot.

Below: *A typical example of '50s commercial photography taken for promotional use, illustrating the uses of the company's products in industry – final inspection of a variable pitch ships propeller.*

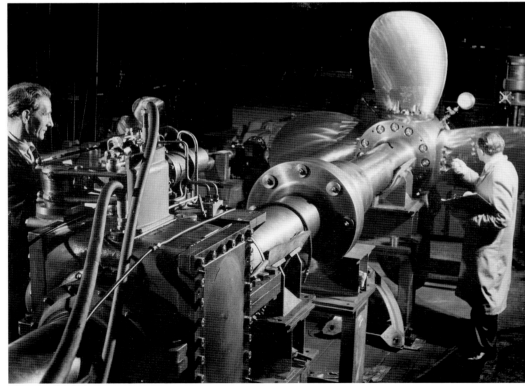

Mobil only entered the petrol market in Britain a year or two before I joined the company and in those early years I worked closely with the company's chief architect as he developed service station design, as above, where experiments with pump island and fascia lighting were being tried out.

Today, a network of pipelines moves fuels from the refinery to inland distribution terminals around the country but back in the fifties, overnight bridging convoys of tankers were used.

When a visit to a service station was quite a leisurely affair while petrol was served, oil checked and the windscreen cleaned.

Right: *From a picture story for the house magazine of one such run, from Coryton Refinery on the Thames estuary to Coventry terminal. As the loaded tankers left Coryton, the empty ones from the previous night's run set off from Coventry, meeting up halfway at a transport cafe where the crews exchanged vehicles before the onward journey in each direction.*

Unloading at Coventry in the early hours. I lit this shot with large flashbulbs, something that 'health and safety' would not allow today with the explosive possibilities! Just as well!

Taking a break from photographing on the Mobil exhibition stand at Farnborough in the late '50s, I was lucky to catch this fly-past of V-bombers – two Valiants flanked by two Vulcans.

Left: *Some different horsepower! For a festive winter issue of the house magazine, a visit to a local brewery and then on to a nearby hostelry where a colleague managed to down a pint from a 'yard of ale' without spilling a drop to go with a piece on drinking vessels down the ages.*

'The Compass''was a glossy magazine circulated to the company's marine customers. It included general interest articles of a maritime nature and this issue from the mid-60s featured the London docks, all soon to close down. This was the first time I had used a helicopter for aerial photography – up until then I had hung out of a single engined Cessna with its door off. I had not allowed for the extra noise of the helicopter and after nearly two hours airborne, again with the door off and in days when headphones were not standard issue, I was quite deaf for the next few days.

Surtees gets off to a flyer and (below) alongside Geoff Duke at the awards ceremony

1959 saw me back photographing motor sport, this time on expenses and with a track pass for the first time. John Surtees, riding for the Italian MV Agusta team and using Mobil fuel and lubricants would, by the end of the year, have won seven World Championships on two wheels in the 350cc and 500cc classes. The venue was the Dundrod circuit, Northern Ireland for the Ulster TT races.

The rear wheel steps out as Surtees accelerates out of the hairpin. Apparently he had been trying to convince the Italian engineers that he needed a smoother power curve and I learned later that he used this shot of mine to convince them of his argument. Within a year he would be moving on to four wheels, leading to his 1964 F1 World Championship, again with an Italian team.

1961

VAUXHALL MOTORS LTD., PUBLIC RELATIONS DIVISION, LUTON, BEDS.

NEWS FROM VAUXHALL

TELEPHONE: LUTON 2600, EX. 2943, 2913 · TELEX: LUTON 82-131/2/3

Further information also from:
Alec Mosley,
Public Relations Officer,
Mobil Oil Company Ltd.
Caxton House, Tothill Street,
Westminster, S.W.1.
Tel: Whitehall 1010

IMMEDIATELY · June 4, 1961.

FOR RELEASE

LONDON-MOSCOW AND BACK BY COACH AT 51.6 MPH

Peter Chapman, a coach operator from Guilsborough, Northamptonshire, braked his 41-seater coach to a halt outside London's Guildhall at 1.08 p.m. today, only 4¾ days after leaving the same spot last Tuesday evening. In the meantime the coach and its passengers had been to Moscow and back.

This record time was achieved in spite of delays of several hours at the Polish customs on both the outward and return journeys. Actual running time for the 3,823-mile return journey was only 72½ hours, which represents an average road speed of 51.6 miles per hour.

YBD 1, the vehicle which made this fastest-ever London-Moscow-London coach journey, was a standard Bedford 41-seater with a luxurious 'Fiesta Continental' body by Yeates of Loughborough. Powered by a standard Bedford diesel engine, the chassis has a 5-speed overdrive top gearbox and a 2-speed axle.

Including a 1300-mile proving run on the Continent just before the Moscow trip began, the coach covered almost 5,000 miles in just over a week, at an average speed of well over 50 m.p.h.

Mr. Chapman, who made the trip to demonstrate his faith in the reliability of this type of British coach for high-speed continental use, said that he thought this was probably the fastest return journey to Moscow ever made from Britain by road.

With Mr. Chapman on the record-breaking trip, which was timed to coincide with the British Trade Fair in Moscow, was a crew of eight. Among these were a photographer, a steward taking a 'busman's holiday' from his normal duties with B.E.A., a reporter and an interpreter.

After leaving Guildhall, London, on the evening of May 30, the coach crossed the Channel on the Dover-Ostend ferry. From there the route lay through Brussels to Helmstedt on the East-German border; then due east, skirting Berlin, to Warsaw, Brest Litovsk, and on through Minsk and Smolensk to Moscow.

./.

While Phil Hill, Wolfgang von Trips and others were setting out to decide the 1961 F1 World Championship, I quite suddenly found myself playing a minor role in a rather different and somewhat slower speed event, but one involving endurance, nevertheless. A high speed coach trip to Moscow and back.

Linking up with Vauxhall Motors who were aiming to show off their latest Bedford coach, Mobil supplied the fuels and lubricants for this demonstration run and never one to miss an opportunity, my boss, the PR manager, volunteered himself and me to join the crew of four drivers, an interpreter and an airline steward to cater for us.

Initially, I was down just to shoot stills but a couple of weeks before the off, it was suggested that I should shoot cine film as well for the Vauxhall film unit hopefully to produce a promotional film. Just one slight problem – I had never handled a cine camera before. Another steep learning curve for me to surmount. While the apprentices at Vauxhall produced a windscreen mounted camera support, I set about learning as much as I could in the short time left before we set off. In the event, the resulting film turned out better than might have been expected, thanks to the skills of the editor and production team and was used extensively by the marketers in both companies. An unknown composer was commissioned to write music specially for it for a very modest sum. Soon after, that same composer hit the big time with his theme for the original black and white Maigret programmes – his name, Ron Grainer.

We arrived in Moscow at about 9.30 in the evening, later than planned owing to a long delay at the Poland-Russia frontier where we were held for hours on the bridge over the River Bug with guards keeping our coach covered by machine guns at each end. Because of that delay, it was decided to make a rapid turn round and set off on the return journey soon after an early breakfast and I was allowed just fifteen minutes in Red Square to get my shots. The instruction was to wait for an official Intourist guide to lead us out of the city but impatience ruled and we set off unaccompanied. Inevitably, we suffered navigational troubles and ended up in a military area. When we were flagged down by a motorcycle sidecar outfit, machine gun at the ready, I felt it prudent to take down my windscreen mounted camera as we were led back to the hotel for questioning. I was left in charge of the parked coach which attracted much attention. A charming young man who said he was an electrician from Georgia came on board and chatted to me in perfect English, taking a more than casual interest in every aspect of our trip. Perhaps he was what he said, or perhaps not ... the KGB comes to mind.

On the outward leg, the Mobil Germany competitions crew met us at Helmstedt on the West-East German border, laying on some refreshments and generally servicing and cleaning the vehicle – a welcome exercise repeated on the return journey.

Enough diesel to get us to Moscow and back to this border crossing was taken on board in drums while our interpreter walked across the short distance to the Communist side to start dealing with the visas and passports. I noted that he crossed safely so decided to follow in order to film the coach coming through – in retrospect a somewhat foolhardy thing to do, festooned with stills and cine cameras as I was. I became aware of border guards taking a great interest in me while easing their weapons into a more ready position but all went well and I was able to rejoin the coach instead of going off to the gulags! As the journey went on, it became apparent that the border crossings had been given notice of what we were about, some expediting our passage but others, as on the Polish-Russian frontier finding every excuse to delay us.

For the period, many of the roads we encountered on the journey were pretty good and presented no problems but in Poland, long stretches were on roads no wider than this with soft shoulders on each side. Oncoming traffic meant running two wheels off the tarmac which tended to be exciting at speed, the drivers reluctant to slow down, as also happened with driver changes when one slid out of the seat as the other slipped in, all at undiminished speed. Out in the country, even in the middle of the night, horse drawn unlit farm carts were another hazard and once, we saw a cow on one side chained to a tree on the other side – fortunately, the chain was slack! Driving through Warsaw at midnight, late night passengers in the trams waved warm greetings to us as they read the message on the coach: 'London-Moscow-London'.

Scenes around Red Square and the Kremlin.

After our false start to the return journey and recall to the city centre while we were checked out, eventually, we were cleared for departure, this time with a guide and once clear of Moscow, set off on the interminable long straights across nothing – just wide open plains, no buildings, trees, anything, not even other traffic. In the middle of the night, the coach suffered a puncture and coming to a halt, the crew got out into total blackness to

begin the task of changing the wheel. I decided that this presented me with an opportunity to walk off down the road to film a shot of the headlights coming through the void. I was careful to make it clear what my plan was and once I had my shot, to ensure they remembered to pick me up. Needless to say, they decided to play a joke on me, driving by and disappearing into the distance. There I was in total darkness with nothing but my cine camera – my passport was on the coach – in the middle of nowhere, except that it was nowhere in Communist Russia. Thankfully, the crew relented and reversed to collect me, thoroughly enjoying my reaction to my predicament. But the delays meant we would spend another night marooned on that bridge over the River Bug.

Fatigue really set in for all of us on that long return journey, apparently I slept for fifteen hours, my body on one side and my legs across the aisle. Our steward had long given up trying to cater for us and it was every man for himself as we raided the food store for whatever was left. In due course, we found ourselves back at the Guildhall, less than five days after setting off, shattered but happy that we had achieved what we had set out to do.

In all, we had completed 3823 miles in just 72.5 hours actual running time, an average speed of 51.60mph. Fuel consumption worked out at 17.2 mpg. These figures never found their way into the Guiness Book of Records, but the trip was unique and achieved its objective, proving the viability and reliability of long distance coach travel.

The BRM of Graham Hill was never far behind Jim Clark's Lotus throughout the 80 lap race but try as he might, the Lotus driver was always in control of the situation.

1964

THE BRITISH AND EUROPEAN GRAND PRIX, BRANDS HATCH

The chance to see this first Grand Prix to be run on the recently extended Brands Hatch circuit was too good to miss after my long break away. I decided to avoid the obvious Paddock Bend and Druids area which had been in place for ten years since the first track extension, instead choosing for the opening laps the dip after Westfield into Dingle Dell.

I was excited by the possibilities offered by the track to feature the sharply changing contours – a welcome change from the relatively flat airfield circuits I was more familiar with. Dingle Dell, lap 1 with Clark's Lotus leading Gurney's Brabham, Graham Hill's BRM, Surtees' Ferrari, Brabham's Brabham, Bandini's Ferrari and McLaren's Cooper.

Jim Clark checks his mirrors as he waits to go out onto the circuit. Most conscientious ... or was he making crafty eye contact with what, in those days, were known as 'pit popsies'? Queuing behind Clark are John Taylor and Phil Hill who appears to be shielding his eyes from the distraction.

Much was expected of Dan Gurney in the second Brabham after his earlier win in the French GP and then winning the 100 bottles of champagne on offer for the fastest driver in the Thursday morning practice. Starting from third on the grid, he quickly moved up to second to challenge Jim Clark for the lead but it was not to be his day. On the third lap, he came into the pits with smoking electrics and was not able to rejoin until the leaders were on lap eight. He finished the race, but still five laps down.

With eyes firmly focused on the car in front, Graham Hill drives a BRM P261 to second place a mere 2.8 seconds behind Clark after 80 laps and 2 hours 15 minutes of close racing with not a single pit stop. Always a firm favourite with British crowds, he won the world championship twice, in 1962 driving for BRM and in 1968 with Lotus. He won Monaco five times and also took victories in the Indianapolis 500 and at Le Mans.

This was the first time that I had the benefit of a track pass, by this time becoming more of a necessity as checks became more stringent.

I particularly enjoyed the challenge of this viewpoint at Hawthorn's. Standing high on the bank, the cars appeared suddenly at high speed and picking them up, following them in the viewfinder and timing the shutter release all happened in little more than a second, a good test of my reactions!

John Surtees speeding round Hawthorn's Bend in the V8 Ferrari 156 to finish a lonely third, not too satisfied with the performance of his car and over a minute behind the Clark-Hill battle. He was the only other driver to complete the full eighty laps.

1964 was to be Surtees formula one championship year – the only driver to win World Championships on two wheels and four and it had been my good fortune to see him performing in both. He joined that other British world champion driving for Ferrari – Mike Hawthorn – in winning the title through consistency, taking victory in only one race to Clark's three, a similar statistic to the 1958 Hawthorn-Moss duel when the figure was one to four.

From his first European race in 1955, 'Black Jack' Brabham soon gained the respect of his fellow competitors both as a talented and a forceful driver and as an intelligent engineer. He would finish fourth in this race with the Climax engined Brabham BT7 after a troubled drive involving two pit stops to check the handling, dropping him behind Bandini in the other works Ferrari for a time.

Jack Brabham would take the world championship three times, in '59 and '60 driving the works Cooper-Climaxes and again, in the car proudly bearing his own name in 1966.

Lorenzo Bandini, who would finish fifth, had the number two Ferrari with the earlier V6 engine while team leader Surtees had the latest V8. The young Italian driver, driving really well, made Brabham work hard to regain his fourth place, keeping him back until the 66th lap. Of the top six in this race, Bandini was the only driver not to be a world champion and he was to die following a crash at Monaco in 1967.

After a small gap, with the leaders already through on the first lap, this group is led by the Cooper-Climax of Phil Hill in eighth place with Ireland (BRP-BRM), Bonnier (Brabham-BRM), Anderson (Brabham-Climax), Hailwood (Lotus-BRM), Ginther (BRM), Spence (Lotus-Climax), Trevor Taylor (Lotus-BRM), John Taylor (Cooper-Ford), Baghetti (BRM), Revson (Lotus-BRM), Maggs (BRM), and Raby (Brabham-BRM) following. Halfway round this first lap, Hill had already made up six places from his fourteenth grid spot.

The fifth of the world champions in this race, Phil Hill (**above**) was now with the works Cooper team led by Bruce McLaren and the best years of his formula one career were already in the past. Taking his world championship in 1961, he was also a three times Le Mans winner with Olivier Gendebien – 58, '61 and '62 – all with Ferrari. Moving back to sports cars and after working with Ford to move their GT project on, he went to Jim Hall's Chaparral concern, bowing out with a fine win back at Brands Hatch in the BOAC 500 in 1967, sharing the drive with Mike Spence.

Looking set to finish higher, Innes Ireland came in only tenth after the engine of his BRP-BRM went off song towards the end of the race.

Among the backmarkers, this two year old Scuderia Centro Sud entered BRM P57 driven by Giancarlo Baghetti. Starting from the back row, he finished twelfth.

Baghetti is best remembered for being the only driver in Formula One history to have won his very first World Championship race. His moment of fame came in 1961 when he had a surprise win in the French Grand Prix at Reims driving a Ferrari 156 entered by a consortium of Italian motor clubs formed to bring on a top class Italian driver. His victory came after the three works Ferraris had either retired or spun down the field and he beat Dan Gurney's Porsche by less than a car's length in an exciting slipstreaming finish. It was to be his only F1 Grand Prix win and the first by an Italian driver since Ascari in 1954.

Bob Anderson, in the third, non-works Brab-ham-Climax, had a fine duel with Phil Hill but eventually had to settle for seventh.

Until Ireland's engine lost power, he had been having a fine scrap with these two, Richie Ginther **(above left)** in the second BRM and Mike Spence **(above)** driving the number two Lotus. At the flag, the BRM had the better of the Lotus, finishing eighth and ninth respectively.

Spence had been drafted into the Lotus team to to replace Peter Arundell, in hospital after a crash at Rouen.

The immortal Jimmy Clark driving perhaps the prettiest 1.5 litre formula one car, the Lotus Climax 25. He won this race but 1964 was not his most successful season – his two championship seasons were 1963 and 1965.

It's thumbs up and a lap of honour for winner Jim Clark, Colin Chapman and Team Lotus mechanics.

The saloon car race was dominated by the Lotus Cortinas of Sir John Whitmore, Jack Sears and Jackie Stewart who finished in that order ahead of a supporting cast of Mini-Coopers and the odd Ford Anglia.

Left: *Leading this group in the supporting GT race is one John Young Stewart, beginning to make a name for himself, driving the Coomb's lightweight E-type Jaguar. Lying second here on the first lap is the AC-Cobra Ford V8 of Jack Sears who wrongly suffered a penalty for a start line mix-up and fought back from seventh place to win, thoroughly trouncing the Jaguar.*

Above: *A great battle for third between David Piper in his beautiful GTO Ferrari and Roy Salvadori in another Cobra came down in favour of the more powerful car.*

1964 RAC RALLY

I had not previously tackled a rally as a subject but shortly before the event, I realised that the first stage of the 'RAC' was to be in Bramshill Forest just south of Bracknell, not too far from home and so I decided to go over to see what I could make of it. Looking back, I feel lucky to have caught a few of the stars of the day, and with so little effort!

Left: *Drifting between the trees, the Healey 3000 of Timo Makinen – always exciting to watch. He finished as runner up to the winning Volvo of Tom Trana.*

Below: *Another of the works Healeys, this one with the Morley brothers, flat out on one of the longer straights.*

Opposite page, clockwise from top left:
One of the many Minis on the rally sweeps through the forest.

The sun shone on the Scandinavian visitors. Volvo driver Olle Dahl raises the dust in a 'Come to Britain' setting.

That most versatile driver, Vic Elford, finished third in his Ford Cortina.

Above: *Fifth was Bengt Soderstrom in a works Ford Cortina.*

Left: *One of the lesser names enjoying the scenery is Fritschy in his Volkswagen Beetle who came in 62nd.*

... *but showing her husband the way home, Pat Moss-Carlsson and Elizabeth Nystrom* **(below)** *came in fourth.*

Two works SAABs:

Mr SAAB himself, Eric Carlsson **(above)** *with navigator Gunnar Palm finished the rally in eighth place ...*

The Mobil Economy Run

Altogether, there were 19 British Mobil Economy Runs, from 1955 to 1973 and others were held in various countries around the world, including the USA where it started. Missing the '55 event, I first became involved in '56 and from there, the event played a major part in my working life until, after the '73 event, it was discontinued just as that year's petrol crisis began to bite and people were queuing at the pumps.

The Run itself was held over three days to cover approximately 1000 miles, 300 to 400 miles each day. Before that, a full day was taken up with the most intensive scrutineering to ensure that every competing car was absolutely standard. In addition to the driver and navigator, each car carried an independent observer whose brief was to ensure that all rules of the road, including speed limits were strictly observed and coasting in neutral was not allowed. There was a limit of forty cars competing in the main event with, in the later Runs an extra ten cars crewed by invited press participants.

The route, which changed each year, was planned to take in all kinds of road conditions from motorways to rural byways in some of the most mountainous and scenic parts of Britain. Route checks and time controls ensured that competitors were kept on their toes and many newcomers to the event would admit to finding it a bigger challenge than expected. This particularly applied to some of the press crews who came along expecting to have a bit of a 'jolly'. Some of them tried to keep it that way but usually their competitive instincts took over as they tried to better the figures achieved by those competing in the Run proper!

By 1962, we had a small unit of three and were developing quite a sophisticated photographic coverage of each run. The task set was to have six or so action shots of each competitor, plus the ten cars in the press section, illustrating the variety and toughness of the route. Add to that, coverage of the pre and post event scrutineering, fuel measurement procedures, route checks and refuelling stops so that typically some five to six hundred shots would be exposed and we would have these ready for the press to make their selection

In the early morning light on a typically difficult section, a Mini climbs out of a Yorkshire village to start another day of economy motoring over a challenging route and against the clock.

by the time the results were announced. This was usually about five hours after the finish once all the fuel measurement and post event scrutineering had taken place. A display of the best prints of the top three in each class would be displayed in the press room with all other shots filed and available for selection by the various correspondents.

With their print orders made and as they moved through to the awards dinner and prize presentation, we would work on so that we could present them with their prints by the coffee and liqueurs stage. To achieve this level of service, the processing and printing arrangements also needed careful planning and varied according to where the Run was based. Many of them started and finished in Harrogate, with the Majestic Hotel as the main centre and where we set up temporary darkrooms. On day one, all three of us would be out shooting on the route, then one would drop out on day two and another on day three to deal with the darkroom work.

Mobil Economy Run

PRESS COVERAGE...

Austin 1100, H. E. Marfleet and D. Dixon, climbing out of Nidderdale. This team won Class II with 47,590 m.p.g. by a narrow margin.

Press Section winners, Brian Sales and Peter Merri... heading for Masham Moor in their Vauxhall Firenza

Above: *Climbing steep hills in wild country and negotiating narrow lanes and streets, all typical Mobil Economy Run territory. Achieving good mpg figures in terrain like this in the North Yorkshire Moors was all part of the challenge.*

Below: *Navigating through a cobbled street in Settle, Yorkshire before dawn, the crew of this Morris Marina startled by our flashes.*

This rock fall was on the Honister Pass in the Lake District, typical of the many hazards encountered along the way.

Keith Duerden shovels snow

FOUR-DAY TREK

THREE weeks before the Route Check on the Run.
Run, Mobil photo- Farther on a puncture
graphers Keith Duerden and called another halt and the
Colin U...
Harrogat...
sance t...

While Mobil sponsored the Economy Run, it was organised on the company's behalf by the Hants & Berks Motor Club which was responsible for every aspect of its organisation – scrutineering and fuel measurement, marshalling route checks and time controls and of special interest to my unit, planning the route. Our task was to check this route out to plan our photographic coverage but with the club only releasing the details early in January and the Run starting in March, it meant that our recce became something akin to a winter rally. We not only had to find the best shots but also work out how to get back ahead of the pack in order to get a second – or even third – location in the day. With the cars starting at two minute intervals, they took about 1hr 45 mins to pass through any given point leaving us with a lot of catching up to do. Often, this meant leaving the official route, which might be on a long loop round and cutting across country to intercept them, involving our own carefully planned and timed itinerary. It was fortunate that the roads were much quieter then, mostly with no speed restrictions outside urban areas and 'safety' cameras were well in the future. Motoring was still very much a pleasure and the recce was always something to eagerly anticipate.

Top: *A press cutting from 'Popular Motoring' magazine.*
Above: *On one very snowy recce, I tried to dig my way through a snow drift climbing out of Swaledale towards Tan Hill. Without success I might add, but we got a bit of publicity out of it!*

It was not only the event itself which achieved wide press coverage. Our small photographic unit had several articles in the professional photographic press through its 28 year existence.

A quote from one in 1973: 'The Run is the most significant event in the Mobil publicity calendar and the Photographic Unit plays an important role in its execution. When I first brought up the subject of the Run at our meeting, a long smile travelled across Keith Duerden's face and in answer to my question, which was something like: 'what exactly does the Unit do in the Economy Run?', 'Have a whale of a time' was the prompt reply'.

For anyone who enjoys motoring, as we certainly did, it provided us with a wonderful opportunity to explore the very best of Britain's most scenic and hilly regions, first on the recce and then on the Run itself. And all with a wonderful excuse to drive enthusiastically – no wonder I had a smile on my face!

They chased forty test cars around the country

(and beat them all to the finishing line)

THE MOBIL ECONOMY RUN is the most important event in the public relations and advertising calendar of Mobil Oil Company Ltd., and the mpg figures achieved by the 40 competing cars form the basis for all the petrol advertising done by the Company. Both before and after the Run, there is a great demand for photographs and it is essential that a full photographic coverage is obtained of every aspect of the five-day event. It is certainly the most important commitment of the year for Mobil's two staff photographers, Keith Duerden and his assistant David Whiting.

From experience gained in previous years, the type of photograph required is known and the basic briefing for the photographers is to obtain at least six really good and varied action shots of each competing car (240-300 shots altogether) which illustrate the toughness of the route. In addition, the scrutineering and fuel measurement procedures which take place before and after the run, and the refuelling stops and route checks during the event, must be well covered. In all, this means that between 600 and 700 black-and-white photographs must be taken. An extra task presented this year was a request from the parent Company in New York for a selection of colour transparencies to use

in their international advertising.

Prints have to be available for the Press immediately the results are known, about five hours after the finish.

To fulfil these requirements, a considerable amount of pre-planning has to be carried out, and as soon as the course of the event (which is different each year) is finalised, Keith Duerden sets out to drive round the route to select suitable locations for scenic and action shots. At the same time, photographically uninteresting stretches are noted so that, where possible, these can be by-passed during the event to enable the photographers to catch up again with the competing cars. It has to be borne in mind that, with 40 cars at two-minute intervals averaging 30 mph, the photographer will then be nearly 1½ hours behind the first car. To make this up over winding and hilly B-class roads necessitates a lot of hard driving.

During the months preceding the event, the Photographic Section finds that, apart from the advance planning, prints of the previous year's Run are required for sales promotion purposes, as references for the design of Start and Finish banners and layout of scrutineering areas and many other purposes. When

Keith Duerden using the Hasselblad to take colour photographs of competitors climbing up to the Hartside Cross route check.

A cutting from one of the magazines which gave us a write up about our activities in 1961.

A scene in Colne, Lancashire, noticed on the recce and to which I just had to return during the event for obvious reasons – two competing Ford Anglias pass by 'Duerdens Yard'.

My parents came from nearby Burnley and Barrowford and my family name is quite common in these parts. Returning many years later, the area had been flattened prior to redevelopment.

Above: *Focusing my camera on a more extreme section than usual, Blue Hills Mine in Cornwall in 1960, better known as a regular stage on the Lands End Trial. and eating a snack while waiting for another car to come into view. The schedule allowed competitors a meal break but we used the time gained to hurry to the next viewpoint.*

Economy against the clock

"We're losing time, we'll have to fly." Were these the words of B. I. Stevens in his Vauxhall Victor 2000?

In the battle to keep to the strict time schedule while using as little petrol as possible, downhill stretches gave drivers the opportunity to ease up their average speed. I nearly took off myself at this point in the North Yorkshire Moors while on the recce and noted it as a likely location for the Run itself. This Vauxhall (above) was not the only one to get all four wheels off the ground but it almost certainly made the highest 'yump'!

On several of the Runs in the '60s., lengthy stages at well known circuits including Oulton and Mallory Parks were included in the itinerary with average speeds of 50-60mph being set, according to the class. Quite a challenge when, at the same time, trying to achieve impressive mpg figures in completely standard cars.

I enjoyed a few laps at Oulton Park in my Triumph Herald while checking the route out before the event.

The weather often played a significant part in making life even more difficult for the drivers trying their best to achieve high mpg figures. It was not just on our reconnaissance trips in January and February that snowfalls would intrude but even as late as March tough conditions could not be ruled out.

This Riley 1.5 driver got away with his slide on a corner in the Trossachs and was able to resume but soon after, another competitor had to retire after a close encounter with the concrete barrier on the outside of the bend. The main picture (left) was later used by the marketers in promotional material – leaflets, point of sale and forecourt display – for de-icers and other winter motoring products.

ECONOMY RUN NEWS

Number Two   March 1966

START

Snow scene in Harrogate at the start of 1965 Economy Run. What was in store this year?

SNOW AND ICE 1965 ECONOMY RUN

Good results in appalling weather conditions

1968—WIND, RAIN, HIGH SPEED AND 50·66 m.p.g!

A RILEY Elf driven by G. Keys from Stone in Staffordshire returned a remarkable 50·66 m.p.g. to win the small car class in the 1968 Mobil Economy Run, which ended in Harrogate in the early hours of Wednesday, 27th March.

This and other results returned by the 40 competitors who battled for three days to use as little petrol as possible over a varied 1,100-mile route, proved again the economy potential of standard production cars.

Only decimal points separated Class I winner G. Keys from the runner-up, H. E. Marfleet from Wirral, Cheshire, who returned 50·05 m.p.g. in a Singer Chamois. It was a ding-dong battle: Keys in the Elf led at the end of the first day, but Marfleet put up a better performance on the race track, so the final result hinged on their performance on the long third day. And, of course, there is no telling what the results in this class would have been, had not B. D. L. R. Smith from Twickenham in Middlesex been disqualified. He went off the road in a tricky section in Wales on the last day in his Reliant Rebel, after leading at the end of the first day and being placed second in the Special Stage at Oulton Park Race Circuit.

J. B. Twort from Reading, Berks, driving a Ford Escort 1300 in Class II for cars of 1,001–1,300 c.c. was a winner from start to finish. He drove immaculately to figure at the top of his class at the end of the first two days and then at the finish another Ford Escort—the 1100 version—driven by W. Baguley from Warrington was close

Geoff Keys, 1968 Class I winner with 50·66 m.p.g. in his Riley Elf, corners hard on this downhill stretch on the Yorkshire Moors.

1800, returned an overall figure of 34·70 m.p.g.

For the second year running the economy potential of the Daimler 2½-litre V8 was demon-

Moving on ...

I first got involved in the company's North Sea activities in the mid-sixties when Mobil was drilling for gas on the Dutch island of Ameland. We took a party of journalists over in a private charter flight to see the operation, giving me my first opportunity to photograph an actual drilling rig in action. As we arrived over the island we noticed with interest that the landing strip was a grass field full of sheep but our pilot was obviously prepared for this eventuality. He swooped the de Havilland Dove in at very low altitude to scatter the sheep to the edge of the field, quickly circled round and landed before they strayed back into our path. This was to give me a foretaste of the increasingly exciting situations I would find myself in as operations in the North Sea developed over the next ten to fifteen years. The Ameland experience was soon followed by the exploration offshore from East Anglia and in addition to the stills photographs, we began shooting film of this work at the request of the parent company for use in an American television programme. That initial footage aroused considerable interest back here and it was decided to develop it into a film of our own. We had been extending the unit's activities to include film production, at first on internal safety and training films but this was our first one intended for wider distribution, especially as an educational tool for schools. The film that emerged, which we called 'Drilling Through Time', showed how the deposits were laid down millions of years ago, leading through to the exploration, discovery and testing of a commercial gas deposit. It was entered into the United States Industrial Film Festival in Chicago where it won a 'Certificate of Excellence for Creativity' – not bad for a film the two of us shot entirely on a 16mm clockwork Bolex cine camera with just fixed lenses and no zoom. This success did much for the standing of our unit and was to lead on to greater things.

In the early '70s, around the time of the Middle East conflict and resulting oil shortages, I went out again to shoot a picture story, this time on the search for oil further north between the Shetlands and Norway. While working on the drill ship Glomar V, once more my luck came into play when the drilling was successful while I was actually on board, resulting in a commercial find which, in due course, was to become the Beryl field. Although there to shoot stills, I had taken my cine camera just in case and was able to shoot the flare as the find was tested **(left)**. This footage was to find its way into our next North Sea film, this time taking the story right through to the first tanker load of crude oil being shipped to the refinery.

Working for an oil company, I found myself being asked why, having found oil in our home waters, motorists were queuing at the pumps and realised that there was a need to explain to the general public that discovery was only the first stage. From there, a production platform had to be designed, built, positioned over the field and then commissioned leading to actual production before the crude oil could be transported to the refinery. I proposed to management that we make a film to do this but it was a year before I got approval. In the meantime, I had joined the editor of 'Mobil World', over from New York, on a trip out to Stavanger in Norway to photograph the production platform under construction.

Civil Engineering

Environmental Design/Engineering
April 1975

SPECIAL REPORT:
offshore construction

On cover:
North Sea's
Condeep
structure
465 ft high

MOBIL NEWS JUNE 1975   MOBIL NEWS JUNE 1975

'The biggest catamaran in the world' being towed into position at Stavanger. In the background on the right of the picture are the three supporting towers of the concrete structure. These are submerged to allow the deck to be floated over and built on.

Witnessing at first hand the enormity of the project in hand made me all the more determined to get the film under way. The platform was to be the first of its kind, known as a 'Condeep' – from 'concrete deep water structure' – in contrast to the more usual all steel construction and in 1975, I found myself going on regular trips over to Norway to film the main stages of construction leading to the eventual tow out into the North Sea.

By the time of that first visit to the construction site in the fjord at Stavanger, the work was already well advanced. From a cluster of eighteen cylindrical tanks, each approximately thirty feet in diameter and 150 feet high, three columns which would eventually support the steel deck section with its drilling rig, production equipment and living accommodation for the crew climbed another 300 feet – an impressive sight from my helicopter camera platform **(left)**. The deck section itself was being built over a hundred miles away round the south coast of Norway at Arendal and when it was ready, would be towed round to be mated with the base. It had been constructed on two redundant oil tanker hulls, making a giant catamaran **(bottom left)**.

As well as helicopters, I had also become used to flying in a small Cessna seaplane for aerial views over in Stavanger. As easy as phoning for a taxi, one would fly in and be at the jetty by the office within ten minutes and I planned to make use of this service to cover the catamaran's voyage from the air, accompanied by Manfred Block, the platform's construction manager. Not everything ran smoothly. Flying over to Arendal, we heard that a thick sea fog had set in there and a landing would not be possible so we diverted to Kristiansand, completing the journey in a rapidly arranged hire car just in time to catch the start of the voyage and get my colleague Colin Underhill on to one of the tugs to shoot surface shots. The next day, reunited with the seaplane, the fog had blanketed the whole area and we spent all day hunting our target, hoping for better visibility but with no luck. Sometimes, coming down below the cloud, the seaplane's floats were nearly skimming the wave tops. At one point, we landed at a tiny coastal village for a break and within minutes were being interviewed, in English, by the local radio station!

Eventually, with fuel running low, our pilot took the decision to return to Stavanger. This involved another flight over the mountains in poor visibility and at times, I realised we were not quite over, but rather alongside some of the higher peaks as their rocky sides emerged out of the gloom a little too close for comfort. Then, we found that it would not be possible to land at our destination as visibility was close to zero. A gap in the clouds revealed a small mountain lake and a rapid descent saw us safely down with little more than ten minutes fuel remaining. The pilot then waded ashore to tie up to a small, stunted tree before returning to give me a pick-a-back, thus saving me getting my feet wet and just in time to catch this shot **(above)** of my gear being carried over by Manfred. Our landing spot was very remote and so we then had to hike a couple of miles across to a small farm we had spotted before landing, where we were able to call for a taxi. It took two hours to find us at the end of this dusty mountain track.

This little episode was but one of many interesting situations encountered during the film's shooting and we certainly had no complaints about life being dull.

Cameramen dicing in Norway

OUR photographers get around quite a bit in the course of duty. They are fairly well inured to things going wrong occasionally, especially weatherwise, but rarely does everything go wrong all the time.

In Norway last month it came very close to that. For a whole week every attempt at filming the *Beryl A* Platform project struck snags. Keith Duerden and Colin Underhill were there to cover the voyage of the largest catamaran in the world, the steel deck section of the platform, from the builder's shipyard at Arendal round the coast to Stavanger. First high winds delayed the deck's departure for three days, so they returned to Stavanger to work on the main concrete structure, only to find heavy rain blanketing the fjord and making shooting impossible. Back to Arendal on the early morning seaplane flight, the pilot cheered them up with reports of bad visibility and so it was to prove. From the southern tip of Norway on, conditions deteriorated rapidly and, unable to find Arendal, the pilot turned back to Kristiansand. A fast drive in a hired car got our men to the shipyard, but an hour after the deck section had set off for the open sea.

Now a powerful launch took Colin on to one of the tugs, his home and camera platform for the next two days, but at times the fog was so thick that the giant deck assembly on its two 20,000-ton tankers was invisible at the end of its towline.

Keith, meanwhile, returned to Kristiansand and the seaplane. Taking off in brilliant sunshine hopes were higher the next morning, but two miles out to sea the fog was as thick as ever. A fruitless search, during which they emerged from under a cloud bank only 25 feet above the sea, had to be abandoned. As the pilot sought a safe route through the mountains in rapidly gathering clouds, a radio message told him that landing at Stavanger was not on as the fog had rolled in there too. With both fuel gauges reading empty, there was no alternative but to make a forced landing on a mountain lake, walk across some fields and phone for a taxi.

Beryl A Platform Construction Manager, Manfred Block, wades ashore after the forced landing carrying the photographer's equipment, callously photographed by Keith Duerden who had been carried off dry-footed by the seaplane pilot.

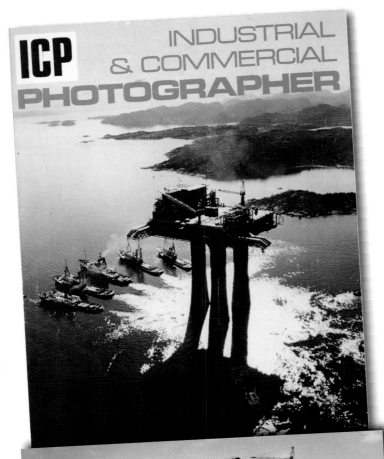

With the platform ready, the delicate task to tow it out of the fjord began. The platform itself was not only the first of its kind to be built, this voyage just beginning was, at the time, the heaviest tow in maritime history and the lead tug, on its maiden task, was the biggest and most powerful up until then. It took two days to reach the open sea and at times, the giant cluster of tanks below the surface was only feet from the underwater rocks, a team of surveyors situated on islets and the shore helping the tow-master, high up on the platform, to steer safely through.

I had about fifteen minutes in the air, during which time I shot film for ITN and BBC news as well as for our own production, plus stills in black and white and colour, an intensive session while sitting at the open door of the helicopter. After that, I transferred to one of the safety boats, the small white vessel, lower right, which was to be my home until the platform was positioned on the field and lowered to the sea bed. It was a privilege to be involved in such a project – special times indeed.

Contrasting conditions in the North Sea, a near flat calm, necessary for the installation of the flare bridge and a drilling rig nearby in a Force 11 storm. It was to be another year before the first tanker load of oil would reach the refinery and the film could be completed.

The writer/producer I worked with was a Morgan enthusiast and had one model from each decade starting with one of the first ever produced.

The film, 'Beneath the North Sea', won five awards at home, in Europe and North America against some much higher budget productions. Translated into several languages, it was used throughout the Mobil world and, an unexpected bonus, went out on the public cinema circuit as a 'B' feature to a Richard Burton film, a pleasing result to add to my small unit's growing record.

Mobil North Sea Film wins a gold

BRITISH SPONSORED FILM FESTIVAL

1978 GOLD AWARD
Category II
BENEATH THE NORTH SEA
Mobil Oil Co. Ltd.
Michael Farlong Films

*Keith Duerden
on location during
filming of "Beneath the North Sea".*

"Beneath the North Sea" — Mobil's new film — the first oil industry picture to tell the complete story of a North Sea oil field from how the deposits were laid down millions of years ago — through exploration and discovery — to production — won a Gold Award at the 1978 British Film Festival sponsored by The British Industrial and Scientific Association.

This award follows a Silver Plaque won at the 13th International Film Festival held in Chicago.

"Beneath the North Sea" has had several weeks public showings through ITC Film Distributors at ABC cinemas in London and in Guernsey and Jersey.

Forward plans include the possibility of featuring it nationally with a new film called "Capricorn One" over the Christmas period.

This dramatic 20 minute picture explains seismic exploration and test drilling from semi-submersible rigs, and goes on to tell the story behind the building, commissioning and installation of the Beryl A platform — the worlds first deep sea oil production unit to use the "condeep" concrete base construction technique.

Beryl A is expected to extract crude oil at peak rates up to 100,000 barrels a day.

The film took two years to make and demonstrated the enormity of the project, the tremendous team effort and the incredibly vast investment needed to bring the discovery of the field "On Stream".

Virtually all the footage for the film was shot by Keith Duerde and Colin Underhill of the Mobil Audio-Visual and Photographic Unit, working at times in what can at best be described as hectic conditions.

Copies of the film are available on hire from
The Mobil Film Library,
Guild Sound and Vision Ltd.,
Woodston House,
Oundle Road, Peterborough,
PE2 9PZ.
The Library reference number for the film is 300 7937 9.

By the early '80s, Mobil had developed the first of the synthetic lubricants, originally launched as Mobil SHC and from which, today's Mobil 1 evolved. My unit was heavily involved in the launch publicity, and my interest was naturally aroused when it was announced that the company would become a sponsor of the Williams team. Driving for Williams, Alan Jones had won the team's first F1 World Championship and in 1981, we produced a marketing film for this new advanced oil. I was able at first hand to witness how the Grand Prix scene had changed.

Although the team themselves, then based in Didcot, gave me every assistance, I was to come face-to-face with the astronomical cost of the essential track passes and the secrecy of operations compared with the casual air of openness in the '50s. It made me appreciate all the more just what a special time I had stumbled into in my younger days. Transport fleets were an important market for the new lubricant and the Williams transporter featured strongly in the film as well as the obvious racing scenes.

To launch the Williams sponsorship, the press were invited to the Coryton Research Laboratories to be addressed by Frank Williams (centre). For this, we had to produce a near lifesize print of the Williams car as a backdrop and (left), a shot in the print laboratory, checking it coming off the line.

This connection also led to a couple of enjoyable days at Donington photographing a sponsored truck race meeting, resulting in this cover shot.

'A JOB TO BE DONE'

Youth projects are seen over a wide area—from the Giant's Causeway in Northern Ireland to the beaches of Cornwall and from the mountains of Cumbria and North Wales to the fens of Cambridgeshire. The film makes it clear that The National Trust owns not just stately homes, but also heathland, mountains, lakes and coast. Rebuilding a heavily eroded path or a dry stone wall, clearing out canal or fen, restoring valuable land or tidying up a beauty spot—these are some of the worthwhile jobs to be done.

'A Job To Be Done' was directed and photographed by Mobil's Chief Photographer, Keith Duerden. Production Associates were Cyril Randell Pictures Limited. It was filmed in Eastman Color and has a running time of 25 minutes.

Copies of this film can be hired from Town & Country Productions Ltd, 21 Cheyne Row, London SW3.

MOBIL OIL COMPANY LIMITED have generously made a new film for The National Trust about young people and the increasing part they are playing in our work.

The considerable cost of the film plus an ample supply of copies for our film library has been entirely met by Mobil. The Trust is extremely grateful to the Chairman, Mr John Loewin, and to the Managing Director, Sir Nevil Macready, and his staff for the personal interest they have taken in this project.

The purpose of the film 'A Job To Be Done' is to stimulate the growing interest among young people in The National Trust and encourage them to lend practical support in its work.

The framework selected for the film is an Acorn Camp, one of about 100 which are organized each year by The National Trust's Junior Division. The purpose of this camp was to continue under export guidance the reconstruction of the eighteenth-century ha-ha at Hanbury Hall in Worcestershire.

Building a stone wall in Derbyshire

(By courtesy of Mobil Oil Ltd)

Weeding and clearing along the Stratford Canal

(By courtesy of Mobil Oil Ltd)

Mobil became involved more and more in a wide variety of sponsorship projects, nearly all of which involved photography in some way, bringing us a whole new range of subjects to work on.

One such was a film we made for the National Trust aimed at involving young people in its restoration and conservation projects. I had the run of the trust's locations from the Giant's Causeway in Northern Ireland right down to Cornwall. Re-building the ha-ha at Hanbury Hall in Worcestershire was one of many places featured (**above**).

Another was for the Royal Life Saving Society, to encourage recruitment to their Lifeguard Units (**right**).

Especially enjoyable was the series of concerts held in the chapel of the Royal Naval College at Greenwich. Yehudi Menuhin

(**above**) was just one of many notable names we were lucky enough to photograph performing there.

"The Protectors"
Mobil CameraTeam's Film

THROUGHOUT most summer weekends last year, Mobil photographers Keith Duerden and Colin Underhill spent their time in company with Life Guard units of the Royal Lifesaving Society, producing and shooting "The Protectors", a film sponsored by Mobil and designed to help Life Guard recruiting.

For several weekends in succession they made abortive visits to Bournemouth where they were frustrated by cold, blustery weather which made filming virtually impossible. They also went to Runnymede on the Thames, to Bridgwater and to Blackpool.

In the end they completed an excellent short film which Keith himself presented to the Life Guards Corps Convention in Christchurch.

Chairman of the Corps, Mr. E. C. Sherwood, has written:

"I am writing to tell you of the very enthusiastic reception given to "The Protectors". Everyone at the Convention was very impressed with the film. We all think it has a touch of genius about it. It is quite different from the normal hum-drum re-

cruiting film and I am inundated with requests for the loan of it already.

"So far Mobil sponsorship has provided a large number of boats, towers, torpedo buoys and these have already resulted in an upward curve in our recruiting graph. I think the effect of the film on recruiting will be even more pronounced."

The film is based throughout on actual experiences of those taking part. A former Thames River Police officer, Les Hughes, who later retired from the Force and went to Bournemouth where he became wholly involved in the work of the Life Guards, is a central figure.

The cast is composed of mainly young people who obviously enjoy themselves immensely while performing a very worthwhile service to the public. We defy anyone with a taste for water sport to see this film without wanting to join in.

16 mm. copies are being distributed to Royal Lifesaving Society Clubs around the country and will be shown at schools, sports clubs and wherever the opportunity occurs to interest people in the work of the Life Guards.

Keith Duerden behind the film camera shoots Les Hughes in the launch on the Thames at Runnymede.

GOODWOOD, SEPTEMBER 1998

Exactly 50 years after attending that first Good-wood meeting in 1948, I was determined to be at the first Revival in '98 and it didn't disappoint. As the day progressed, there was the 'Thin Wall Special' and a 250F Maserati **(right)** and then Stirling Moss, instantly recognisable at the wheel of an Aston Martin DBR1 **(below)** and the '58 'Vanwall' **(below right)**. While my camera was rather more sophisticated than those I used earlier, I shot on black and white film of course – what else?

It was good to be back.

Attending that first Goodwood Revival had its own revival effect on me. I had not been back to Prescott since my RAF days in 1951 when I took this shot (lower left) of J Blomfield climbing the hill in his Bugatti.

Tyre barriers and armco now line the corners, the trees have put on a bit of extra girth and of course, the drivers' headgear has changed from beret to crash helmet but just as at Goodwood, the scene looked remarkably similar, if somewhat smarter, on my return at a VSCC meeting.

A first visit to Shelsley Walsh and classic meetings at Silverstone have followed and naturally the Goodwood Revival is a regular fixture for me. The opening race on the Saturday morning with ERAs in full-on drifts through Madgwick is a great start to the event.

It was Roy Salvadori who said 'give me Goodwood on a summer day and you can keep the rest of the world'.

And taking me back to where it all started for me as a schoolboy with that Bira book and my first camera, one of Bira's 1930s ERA twins, 'Remus', can be seen regularly, now in the hands of Ludovic Lindsay.

Around the time I retired from active professional photography in 1997, I recall being pleased that traditional silver image making – film and sometimes, even glass plates in the early days – had seen me through my career. Digital photography had by then been around for some time although quality at affordable cost still had some way to go. But then, as I was encouraged to dig out my photographs to make them available for others to see, the timing coincided with the coming of age of digital photography, making their restoration a real possibility and eventually leading to the publication of this book.

With much needed help, acknowledged earlier, I found myself on another 'learning curve' of computers and scanners as I prepared them, in the first place for the web. Exploring my disorganised archive became an enjoyable challenge as I felt my way into this new world of digital imaging technology. At the same time, it revived my own memories of this special period in motor racing and how my unplanned activities then, helped shape my future career.

As a treat for Mobil dealers, a day at Silverstone was laid on in 1984, complete with two Porsche 956s, every guest being taken round for three high speed laps. After everyone had their turn, I was allowed my own special thrill, Jonathon Palmer my chauffeur in the Canon Porsche. My abiding memory is not just of the outright speed, approaching 200 mph down Hangar Straight, but it was the cornering speed which was to leave the most lasting impression. I recall having the widest smile on my face after my turn! In similar vein, just one lap of Goodwood in a Ferrari 250 SWB with none other than my hero from earlier days, Stirling Moss at the wheel. Making that experience even more special, the car, 'RU15', was owned at the time by my friend from schooldays, Michael Hall, with whom I had shared so many good times at those very early meetings in the forties and fifties.

Right: *In the Goodwood paddock recently, I was reunited with the Rob Walker Connaught of 1952/53 which, along with the boys from Pippbrook Garage had played such a part in helping me gain access to pits, paddock and starting grids back in the '50s. It was pleasing to see that my polishing of some fifty years earlier had not been neglected.*